One Foot in
Heaven

Growing Older and Living to the Full

Michael Hare Duke

TRIANGLE

Published in Great Britain in 2001 by
Triangle
SPCK
Holy Trinity Church
Marylebone Road
London NW1 4DU

Scripture quotations are from:
New International Version, copyright © 1973, 1978, 1984 by
International Bible Society. Used by permission of
Hodder & Stoughton Ltd, a member of the Hodder Headline Plc Group.
New Jerusalem Bible, copyright © Darton Longman & Todd Ltd,
1 Spencer Court, 140–142 Wandsworth High Street, London SW18 4JJ.

British Library Cataloguing-in-Publication Data

A catalogue record for this book is available from the British Library

ISBN 0-281-05399-5

Typeset by Pioneer Associates, Perthshire
Printed in Great Britain by
Omnia Books, Glasgow

One Foot in Heaven

Michael Hare Duke was born in Calcutta in 1925. At 18 months he and his older sister returned to England and were left in the care of a devoted nanny. His education eventually took him to Bradfield College and Trinity, Oxford. Between these two he served from 1944 to 1946 in the RNVR. He trained for the ministry at Westcott House, Cambridge, and was ordained in the London diocese to serve as a curate in St John's Wood. He spent six years as vicar of St Mark's, Bury, and then went as the first Pastoral director of the Clinical Theology Association in Nottingham. In 1964 he combined the psychological task with pastoral work as vicar of St Paul's, Daybrook. In 1969 he was elected Bishop of St Andrew, Dunkeld and Dunblane in the Scottish Episcopal Church, where he served for 25 years.

On his retirement he was elected chairman of Age Concern Scotland where he remained for the maximum two years of office. He now chairs the National Forum on Older Volunteering, supported by CSV and RSVP (Retired and Senior Volunteer Programme).

He has been married for 51 years has four children and ten grandchildren.

'No man is an island', and no author is a one-man band, certainly not this one. I have been taught so much about old age by colleagues and staff at Age Concern Scotland, especially its director, Maureen O'Neill. The professionalism of the SPCK staff has kept me right in preparing the manuscript, and friends have made sure that I was rescued from the pitfalls dug by my computer. Naomi Cathryn has been tireless in pursuing references and permissions. Friends and family have been patient with the time that I have consumed in thinking, writing and discussing. It has realistically been a combined operation.

Contents

Acknowledgements and References

Albom, Mitchell (1997), *Tuesdays with Morrie*, Little, Brown.
Barker, P. (1996), *The Ghost Road*, Vol. 3 of Regeneration Trilogy, Penguin.
Berger, P. (1970), *A Rumour of Angels*, Penguin Books.
The Dead Citizens Charter (1998), The National Funerals College.
Donne, John (1660), *Sermons*.
Ebrahim, Shah (2000), letter in *British Medical Journal*, Vol. 320, p. 1205.
Eliot, T. S. (1963), *Collected Poems 1909–1962*, Faber & Faber.
Erikson, Erik (1965), *Childhood and Society*, Penguin Books.
Furlong, Monica (1991), 'Being Human', in Hare Duke (1991) pp. 105–6.
Grenfell, J. (1939), 'Into Battle', first published, *The Times* 28 May 1915, in Quiller Couch, ed., *Oxford Book of English Verse 1250–1918*, p. 1135.
Hare Duke, Michael (1991), ed., *Praying for Peace*, Fount.
Hare Duke, Michael (1994), *Hearing the Stranger*, Cairns Press.
Heidegger, M. (1967), *Being and Time*, Oxford University Press.
Jones, Noragh (1994), *Power of Raven, Wisdom of Serpent*, Floris Books.
Küng, Hans (1995), *A Dignified Dying*, SCM Press.
Moody, Raymond (1975), *Life After Life*, Corgi Books.
Parsloe, Phyllida (1999), 'Some Spiritual and Ethical Issues in Community Care for Frail Elderly People', in Jewell, ed., *Spirituality and Ageing*, Jessica Kingsley, p. 140.
Post, Stephen (1995), *The Moral Challenge of Alzheimer Disease*, Johns Hopkins Press.
Pritchard, Jacki (1999), ed., *Elder Abuse Work. Best Practice in Britain and Canada*, Jessica Kingsley.

Rinpoche, Sogyal (1998), *The Tibetan Book of Living and Dying*, Rider.

Roberts, Karen (1994), *Becoming Attached*, Warner Books.

Report (1999), Royal Commission on Long Term Care, *With Respect to Old Age*, The Stationery Office.

Schama, Simon (2001), *A History of Britain*, BBC Worldwide.

Shaw, G. B. (1921), *Back to Methuselah*, Constable.

Thich Nhat Hanh (1993), *Present Moment, Wonderful Moment*, Rider.

Thomas, Dylan (1952), *Collected Poems 1934–1952*, J. M. Dent & Sons.

Tillich, Paul (1952), *The Courage to Be*, Nisbet.

Wallace, Paul (1999), *Agequake*, Nicholas Brealey Publishing.

Winnicott, D. W. (1964), *The Child, the Family and the Outside World*, Penguin Books.

Worden, William (1991), *Grief Counselling and Grief Therapy*, Routledge.

Yalom, Irvin D. (1991), *Love's Executioner and Other Tales of Psychotherapy*, Penguin.

Foreword

Bishop Michael Hare Duke has been the Chairman of Age Concern Scotland for a number of years. That he has produced a book of this scope at the end of his time in office, drawing on his very broad experiences, is to be welcomed. He tackles the hard issues relating to growing old, and emphasizes the need to have fun.

The population is growing older. This is a cause for celebration, but also for being aware that extended older age brings with it some particular issues, including problems of health and bereavement. But it is important to recognize that old age is as diverse and complicated as youth – opportunities exist for a fulfilling life for those who wish to take them and whose life circumstances allow them.

This book looks at the issues of what we mean by old age, so variously defined by politicians and society in general, and it examines how we feel after that barrier of retirement. It considers the potential for personal growth in the third and fourth ages and the role of faith at a time when it is possible to reflect on achievements or failures in life.

The book provides unique insights and will be a welcome addition to the debate on an ageing society.

Maureen O'Neill
Director, Age Concern Scotland

1

What is Old Age?

My grandfather, a Church of Ireland clergyman, was born in 1815. His first marriage was childless and aged 65 he married Jemima Coates, a young woman 34 years his junior. Between 1877 and 1893 they had a family of seven children, six of whom survived into adult life, dying between the ages of 60 and 100 years old.

Canon Duke, as he became, died in 1905, still in harness as the Vicar of the parish of Glencraig in Co. Down. His diary for 1885 shows him vigorously pursuing the affairs of the parish and travelling into Belfast for clergy meetings. At the age of 70 he gave no evidence of feeling that he was old. To his children, however, he was a strange, enigmatic figure who was thought to pray out loud in Hebrew while striding up and down in his study. His heavily Protestant prejudices against the Church of Rome are documented in his Bible that contains all the notes for his sermons. Against 'the mark of the beast' in the book of Revelation, he has written the name 'W. E. Gladstone', presumably because of his support for Catholic toleration in Ireland. These views seem to have been absorbed without discussion by the family and gave a strong sectarian bias to their opinions throughout their lives. In this they reflected the model of unquestioning respect for the elders which was the norm at that time.

After her husband's death Jemima appears in family photographs dressed not only as a widow but as an old lady in spite of being only 56 years old. Age was clearly a matter of how you perceived yourself or were perceived by family and friends.

More generally the appearance, behaviour and role of the older members were subjects dictated within a particular section of society. Being old as an occupant of the 'Big House' or even the Rectory was very different from the experience of the mill-worker or the miner. Nevertheless there were agreed assumptions about what age required. Fashion and deportment combined to suggest that for the older person the years of innovation were past and now life-style should be based on the expected health, mobility and politics of class. 'Old age' was primarily a social role and its contribution was to maintain the fabric of society and help the differing generations cohere.

Within the last century there has been a major shift in population numbers which has changed the relationships between the generations and requires a new assessment of age. The relative numbers of old and young have been reversed. Once it could always be assumed that the children of a population outnumbered the grandparents. Now the traditional pyramid of population has been inverted. As the generation of the baby-boomers begins to move into middle age, the pattern of fertility is decreasing. In order for a population to remain stable it requires each woman to produce 2.1 children. In the 1990s the birth-rate in 61 countries in which almost half of the world's population lives was already at or below that level. By around 2010, a further 28 countries, including India, Indonesia and Egypt, are expected to follow suit (Wallace, 1999). In the UK it is predicted that by the year AD 2040 the number of those under 20 will have fallen by two million while those over 60 will have grown by twice that number. Specifically those over 100 years old will increase from 300 around 1950 to 3,600 a century later.

The overall effect on world population statistics is that the old fear of overpopulation will have receded and be replaced by the worry of reduction. 'Populations in Europe are poised to plunge on a scale not seen since the Black Death in 1348' (Wallace, 1999). The effects of this are likely to be felt throughout society, in economics, especially in pensions and investment, in housing. Most immediately the political sphere will be shaken: 20 per cent of the electorate is now over 60 and set to increase. This means that grey power has come of age. As manifestos are drawn up for elections it will become increasingly important to recognize that 'age counts'.

But in what way will this influence be used? It has been the custom for political lobbies to flex their muscles to seek their own advantage or protect their own rights at the expense of others. Because old age is beginning to be seen in a new light, is it possible that elders can reflect on their responsibility to seek fair shares for all? Could grandparents be trustees for the next generation and not operate in solidarity with their peer group alone? Secondly, employment will require more older people to stay at their jobs instead of the tendency to encourage early retirement to make way for younger employees. The age shift has begun to demand a rethinking of the word 'old'. In the past it has meant by implication 'infirm', 'less useful', 'expendable'. As more people are living to a greater age, the definitions are being revised. For instance, the instruction found on the hospital notes of an elderly woman patient NFR (not for resuscitation) caused public indignation, whereas, a generation or so earlier, it might have been unremarked or else assumed to be common practice. Writing in the *British Medical Journal*, Professor Shah Ebrahim of the Department of Social Medicine, Bristol University argued, 'Our attempts over the past three decades to produce humane doctors and nurses capable of responding to patients' needs regardless of age have not been rewarded.' The article concludes, 'The first step in making progress is to acknowledge – at the highest level – that stereotyping on the basis of age exists and is unjust' (Ebrahim, 2000).

In many other ways old age is a new country. The rise in population numbers is partly due to the advances in medical care which have given human beings a revolutionary control over sickness and death. Medicine and surgery have found remedies for conditions that in an earlier age would have proved fatal. Antibiotics, heart surgery, transplants, intensive care, joint replacements and many other interventions have allowed people to play God, choosing to fight off death, extend human life and improve its quality. Leisure opportunities have been enhanced; new horizons have opened on food and drink; through the new information technology there is an enlarged awareness of the world and a knowledge of both opportunities and threats on a global scale.

In 1921 George Bernard Shaw wrote a play, *Back to Methuselah*, which was strangely prophetic of such new dimensions. The plot centred round the notion that Creative Evolution might reverse the trend that had brought down the expectation of life from the unbelievable age of the patriarchs in the Book of Genesis to a mere 'three score years and ten'. In the light of the post-war reflections of the 1920s, it seemed, Shaw argued, that if the human race were to survive, its members would require considerably more years than the present span to mature so that their childish aggression could to find a way of expression that was better than competition and militarism. Just as the centipede had developed its numerous legs because it needed them, so humankind for its own survival might need to increase its longevity to allow its members time to mature into world statesmen capable of handling the complexity of the modern world. If this sounded plausible in the 1920s, the demands of the twenty-first century with the problems that arise from globalization and the information explosion have reinforced the need for some way in which the adult mind can expand to encompass the multiplicity of issues involved in decision-making.

Shaw begins his argument with a scene in which Adam and Eve reflect on the prospect of immortality in the Garden of Eden.

Eve: You sometimes sit for hours brooding and silent, hating me in your heart. When I ask you what I have done to you, you say you are not thinking of me but of the horror of having to be here for ever. But I know very well that what you mean is the horror of having to be here with me for ever.

Adam: Oh! that is what you think, is it? Well, you are wrong. It is the horror of having to be with myself for ever. I like you; but I do not like myself. I want to be different; to be better, to begin again and again; to shed myself as a snake sheds its skin. I am tired of myself. And yet I must endure myself, not for a day or for many days, but for ever. That is a dreadful thought.

A dialogue follows with the Serpent concerning time and death. Eventually the serpent advises, 'Choose a day for your death; and resolve to die on that day. Then death is no longer uncertain but certain.' In this way Adam becomes committed to a life-span of a thousand years.

Shaw then moves the action to the second decade of the twentieth century. Two brothers, one a professor of biology, the other an ex-clergyman are discussing the question of longevity. Their conclusion is that the human life as it is experienced trivializes every commitment. Using Shaw's interpretation of Darwinism they postulate that by exercise of human will, the expected life-span of the whole population could be prolonged. When this begins to happen the play speculates about the con-flicts that might arise between those who represent the longevity of the future and the people who will continue to die in their seventies. The dialogue is designed to reflect the way that society is constructed with certain expectations; if these are subverted, chaos or conflict is the result. Shaw's conviction is that human beings will not be cured of their aggression by the gift of years, they will merely shift the form of their complaints. The action moves to the year AD 3000 and in the final act to AD 31,920. The tension is between the ancients who are into their second and third centuries and the 'adolescents' still around one hundred years old. It centres round the understanding of what is worth-while. The ancients have grown uninterested in the enjoyments of youth, 'dancing, singing, mating' which become 'unsatisfying after a while'. Instead they lay claim to a level of experience that is way beyond the 'young'. When one of the 'youth' chal-lenges an ancient about the apparently miserable quality of his life he is met with the reply: 'Infant: one moment of the ecstasy of life as we live it would strike you dead.'

Shaw is making the point that the changing expectations of life govern the relation between the generations. For the Ancients the immediate pleasures of the senses have palled and the expectation of a greater life span has taken them to other interests. Unfortunately he does not question the idea that the Ancients are still engaged in the same dynamics of rivalry as ever. It does not occur to him that this might be one of the characteristics to be outgrown.

Shaw sums up that differences that he imagines would occur in a dialogue between a 'Youth' in his first century and a 'Maiden' in her second. He accuses her of no longer loving him and she replies:

> Just think. I have hundreds of years to live: perhaps thousands. Do you suppose I can spend centuries dancing, listening to flutes ringing changes on a few tunes and a few notes; raving about the beauty of a few pillars and arches; making jingles with words; lying about with your arms round me, which is really neither comfortable nor convenient; everlastingly choosing colours for dresses, and putting them on, and washing; making a business of sitting together at fixed hours to absorb our nourishment; taking little poisons with it to make us delirious enough to imagine we are enjoying ourselves; and then having to pass the nights in shelters lying in cots and losing half our lives in a state of unconsciousness. Sleep is a shameful thing: I have not slept at all for weeks past. I have stolen out at night when you were all lying insensible – quite disgusting I call it – and wandered about the woods thinking, thinking, thinking; grasping the world; taking it to pieces; building it up again; devising methods; planning experiments to test the methods; and having a glorious time. Every morning I have come back here with greater and greater reluctance; and I know that the time will soon come – perhaps it has come already – when I shall not come back at all.

> The Youth (Strephon): How horribly cold and uncomfortable!

> The Maiden: Oh, don't talk to me of comfort. Life is not worth living if you have to bother about comfort. Comfort makes winter a torture, spring an illness, summer an oppression, and autumn only a respite.

> (Shaw, 1921)

The dialogue is setting out a new perspective on life derived from the fact that the maiden is 'growing up', but after a century of experience. The Ancients who overhear the conversation approve, taking her side against the demands of the Youth. The situation at the end of the twentieth century is beginning to reflect a similar shift of attitudes, although not in the proportions that Shaw's plot suggested. The recent book *Agequake* by Paul Wallace to which we have already referred sets out the revolution in population statistics and their likely effect. There are other social implications which he has not mentioned. For instance, it is commonplace to deplore the breakdown of marriage at the end of the present century. If notice is taken of statistics, however, the number of people who ended up married to the same partner with whom they had started was not far different one hundred years ago, from today's rates. The high numbers of death in childbirth and the general low level of life-expectancy substituted death for divorce as the agency which put couples asunder. In addition, as expectations of the quality of the marriage relationship have risen, it is not surprising that couples fail to achieve the standard which is further enhanced by the expectation that the marriage has a greater potential for survival over an increased number of years. Age alters values and the shift has already begun to occur, not because the present generation are more irresponsible but because the new circumstances have changed the expectations.

In the light of the shifts produced by the new population scene, two careful pieces of analysis have been undertaken. First, the United Nations declared 1999/2000 the International Year of The Older Person and from this arose discussion in which statistics, attitudes and expectations were reviewed. Second, Age Concern, in the same period, have conducted a Millennium Debate of the Age to set an agenda for British society in relation to its older members.

Both of these bodies are united in their conviction that the increasing number of people who are expected to live much longer is not primarily a matter for alarm. The popular press have used the language of 'a time bomb'; old age has been seen as a threat to a stable society and the images of age have been negative rather than positive. Social policy has also perceived elderly employees as a liability and stereotyped them as unable to learn new skills or handle new technology. These are all attitudes which a healthy society needs to challenge, in particular the suggestion that age is a kind of disease or that it is an adequate diagnosis for any deteriorating functions with which older patients present. New opportunities, not problems, are arising. Because this has never happened before unique responses are required politically and socially. Planners, economists, educationalists and politicians are challenged to think new thoughts. So are the leaders of all the world religions. It is no longer enough to say as one poet wrote in the Psalms: 'To the Lord our God belong the issues of life and death.' Medical science has found ways both of overcoming infertility and deferring the time of death. Human beings must now learn to exercise their new-found powers responsibly towards each other and the earth's inhabitants as a whole. No human group and no natural species should be exploited. The liberty or rights of others must not be taken away by those whose scientific knowledge, wealth or political authority has brought them new power. Instead they have in their turn to find a new obedience to the task of creating a sustainable society.

This left little room for decisions which to-day might be called 'responsible parenthood'. The Scriptural command was 'Go forth and multiply'. In the light of the experience of infant mortality no questions were asked about how many mouths the available land could feed, what scale of population the village could sustain or whether the globe was becoming overloaded.

The assumptions have now changed. Parenthood has been privatized to become either a personal right where it is desired, or an issue of individual decision in the light of career development. The societal dimension, which would urge that either it might be a duty to build up the strength of the nation or that procreation might be a social, political or environmental time bomb, is ignored.

When Age Concern mounted its major exercise of the Debate of the Age throughout England, Scotland, Wales and

Northern Ireland, a wide-ranging series of meetings identified five clusters of topics to be addressed:

1. Values and attitudes (including decisions about the end of life)
2. Work and life-styles (including ageism at work)
3. Paying for age (state finance or private contributions)
4. Health and care
5. Built environment and transport (housing for old age and the maintenance of community)

These had some correlation with the themes which were chosen for the International Year of The Older Person where the five principles of :

1. Independence
2. Participation
3. Care
4. Self-fulfilment
5. Dignity

were highlighted as a guide to all that was undertaken by the State or voluntary bodies and non-governmental organizations.

In whatever way the lists are made up, the fundamental needs remain similar. The value accorded to older people must take into account their rights as human beings and must give them a chance to develop emotionally, intellectually and spiritually throughout their lives, as much in their later years as in youth. They also need to be free from anxiety about paying for residential care if they need it, find themselves sharing in a congenial community and encouraged to value themselves in relation to the needs of others. This involves establishing a careful balance between individual rights, corporate needs and overall sustainability.

The concrete ways in which 'dignity' needs to be expressed were spelled out in the paper on Values and Attitudes. It argued that action should be taken by the Government to achieve them, including:

1. Equal opportunities legislation for the employment of older people
2. Pensions raised to the same level as the Minimum Income Guarantee
3. A National Care Standards Commission to ensure sufficient resources for residential care
4. Public transport provision to be improved
5. Health care resources not to be rationed on the basis of age. Palliative care to be available to all to ensure a dignified death
6. Health promotion schemes to encourage healthy life-styles and reduce the period of ill-health towards the end of life

Although these recommendations are readily accepted in principle, when it comes to putting them into practice, difficulties arise. Two issues need to be addressed highlighting the tensions that can arise between the ideals of 'participation' and 'care' when the choice of an individual can be in conflict with the generally accepted notion of care.

A prime example is the controversy which surrounds the definition of 'a dignified death'. On one hand this might include legislation that avoided the right to protracted care for a person when the quality of their life had gone; on the other hand there is a fear that it might legitimize euthanasia. Some religious viewpoints argue against any relaxing of the law that might make it possible for doctors with the consent of a relative to switch off a life-support machine or withdraw artificial means of feeding. There have been controversies about withdrawing life-support systems from those who have been agreed by medical judgement to be 'brain dead' or in a persistent vegetative state. Is there a danger that 'care' which seeks to end a life of intolerable pain or distress could open the way to murder? How can a boundary be held between the two forms of death? The question makes some lawyers anxious. Because of this uncertainty, the medical profession may continue to treat a patient beyond the point when common sense would suggest that enough was enough.

I had a little dog who was very old and whose kidneys had

begun to fail. I was impressed by the advice of the vet who said, 'He's dodging along and quite happy, let's not put him through unnecessary treatment.' He died undisturbed but perhaps a little earlier than might have been the case if we had taken action. When faced with the suggestion by my own doctor that various symptoms I was displaying should be investigated at the hospital, I quoted the vet and was met with stern disapproval by the doctor! I was grateful for his personal concern, but there must be cases where it is relevant to ask whose anxieties are being treated by some medical interventions – the patient's, the relatives' or the doctor's?

Second, because many of these recommendations require additional expenditure from a limited budget, there can be competition for scarce resources. Sometimes this can become a political issue. When public spending has to be divided between education, employment, health and environment, how big a slice ought to be allocated to old people's welfare? Even within the health care sphere it is a complicated calculation with a variety of factors in the equation. There is the direct cost of the treatment. What is the likely outcome, will it offer the promise of long-term cure or short-term alleviation? Who represents the patient's wishes? Are these to maximize comfort and reduce the pain or to undergo anything that will give a few additional months or weeks of life? The wider society must ask, 'if this person is treated who will have to be denied?'

There can be a similar tension within a family. Western societies are aware of bad practices in the financial abuse of older people by their relatives. Children are exploiting parents or grandparents, misusing the power of attorney to gain control of money or property that belongs to older people, refusing to release money to pay for care because they hope to inherit it. If this can happen within a family, it is possible that intergenerational conflict may develop within society and older people be denied their rights. In Canada legal procedures are in place to protect the elderly. The Scottish Parliament has enacted a new Incapacity Bill which is concerned to give similar protection to all vulnerable people.

Age Concern is confronting the problem and is involved in an educational programme about all forms of elder abuse, particularly in its psychological and financial forms.

If we are to take seriously the aim of according dignity to every old person this must also include a recognition of his or her ethnic origin and a respect for it. On a broad level there can be a danger that the country of origin will weigh against their rights and so justice be denied. Alternatively an inverted prejudice could tip the scales in their favour for fear of incurring an accusation of racism. This in its turn could produce an institutionalized resentment. In a more practical way an educational programme is required to ensure that misunderstandings do not arise from a lack of knowledge across cultural boundaries. For instance, the dietary needs of some minorities differ from those of the majority. If these are overlooked in hospitals or other care institutions they can cause resentment. A harassed nurse may not see the significance of a piece of ham included on the plate of a Jewish or Muslim patient. 'Push it to one side and ignore it' may seem an obvious solution, yet this fails to realize that all the contents of the plate are now contaminated. Such a misunderstanding can lead to a whole world of bad feeling on both sides. 'Fussy, ungrateful old thing,' thinks one; 'She is belittling my religion,' thinks the other. Stereotypes can be set up which will colour attitudes for years.

Another instance is that at the times of death quite different rituals are required by different faith communities. An insensitive approach can cause deep distress. This requires training for all those concerned so that they know the facts of what various traditions expect, and also are aware that spiritual care must listen to the music behind the words when halting questions are asked or fear produces embarrassed or trivial comments.

This evidence highlights the fact that within our culture we need a change of attitude to old people which is more than the passing of resolutions. It is not enough to reaffirm old values; the new demographic situation requires a shift from the perception of old people as objects of charitable goodwill to understanding them as powerful contributors to society. The value placed upon older people should make it unthinkable to mistreat them. Within Britain a high proportion of voluntary care of the old is undertaken by people who are themselves in the older age brackets. As grandparents they help their children with the grandchildren and within the wider community they provide an important link between the generations. They also carry the stories of the earlier days, and children want to learn not only the memories that people enshrine but also to hear of their views about values which may well be in contrast to the prevailing norms of society.

As part of the British Government's response to the International Year of The Older Person, a Royal Commission on Long Term Care was appointed in 1997 under the chairmanship of Professor Sir Stewart Sutherland. Its Report *With Respect to Old Age* appeared in 1999. Its underlying philosophy was summed up: 'The moral test of Government is how that Government treats those who are in the dawn of life, the children, those who are in the twilight of life, the elderly, and those who are in the shadows of life – the sick, the needy and the handicapped.' The Report goes on to affirm that

> there is now a clear opportunity to see old age for what it is, a stage of life where we have the gift of time to be able to acquire knowledge and experiences for which there may not have been time during working lives. In this age of opportunity while physical capabilities or mental faculties may change, people should not necessarily be assumed to be passive recipients of the goodwill of others or inevitably incapacitated, befuddled or redundant. Society should recognize the value inherent in older people and the value to society in using its ingenuity to help older people to continue to realise their potential more effectively. (Report, 1999, 1.14)

This is an encouraging cost-benefit analysis to reinforce a moral conclusion.

These conclusions have been reinforced for me at a personal level by conversations with my own grandchildren. Sometimes, as the result of a form history project at school, there will be a telephone call asking for details of my experiences in the Second

World War. A more generic enquiry may be phrased: 'What was it like in olden times, Grandfather?' This may be a ten-year-old tapping into my personal memories. Via myself she can discover what I was told by my parents which covers a span of more than a century. Another aspect of learning between generations is that as new theories of child-rearing or social management emerge, those with long memories may be able to provide helpful contrasts between past and present.

With regard to the needs of older people, pensions, housing, transport and all the other supports of practical living should not be ignored, but behind these there lie the questions that haunt us all as we grow older. How do I forgive myself or others for the past? What have I achieved? What happens next? How these issues are resolved will determine how comfortable a person is with old age.

This is especially important because contemporary advertising seems designed to give the impression that a person over 65 is not really valued. Either you are advised to invest in the kind of ointment that will protect you from the wrinkles of age or else the young and glamorous seem to be the only age group that can say 'I'm worth it!' In either case the message is that youth and beauty are the only real assets, so hold on to them while you can. Perhaps this explains why for old people so much resentment is focused on the level of the state pension. Everything in our society is assigned a cash value, but perhaps the older generation should not acquiesce in this misguided attitude but realize that they have a priceless witness to give to the riches of friendship and respect. When this is understood they will not look for a cheque in the post so much as an expression of gratitude that builds good relationships.

Every community needs to examine the assumptions that lie behind its priorities. As well as economic decisions, strategies are required to change attitudes, using education, the arts, particularly drama, the news media, the churches and all who have access to a wide public. Where do older people look for allies in the task of building a better society? How do they find the resources within themselves? The first requires an understanding of sociology, the other of spirituality. It is to the latter with its many dimensions, artistic, affectionate, musical, poetic and far from exclusively religious that the rest of this book will be devoted. It is only from within senior citizens themselves that the answer will come to the question 'What is old age?' They will confirm or reject public programmes and build a community in which they feel at home and find a sense of purpose as active citizens, whatever the number of years with which they are credited at their next birthday.

2

The Twilit Frontier

There is an essential ambivalence about ageing. It is a process that begins as soon as we are born and it only ceases when we die. It is therefore an integral part of human existence. 'Growing up', getting older, is something to which children look forward. Even later in life it brings a new status. The old may be assumed to have the wisdom of experience; they have weathered the storms of life and achieved a balanced tranquillity; grey hairs are to be respected. Yet at the same time there is an unattractive quality summed up in the speech of the melancholy Jaques in *As You Like It* describing the seven ages of man:

> And so from hour to hour we ripe and ripe,
> and then from hour to hour we rot and rot.

The view is reinforced by lines from *The Passionate Pilgrim*, a collection of verse published in 1599.

> Age, I do abhor thee, youth I do adore thee.

And

> Crabbed age and youth cannot live together:
> Youth is full of pleasure, age is full of care.

The contrast suggests that, while old age is inevitable, youth is where people really want to be. This view of age partly reflects the culture of Shakespeare's day. The reign of Queen Elizabeth I belonged to the young. It was a time of exploration, of military and naval daring and Renaissance enthusiasm in art and drama. Elizabeth as Queen embodied the image of her age.

The older she got, the younger her portraitists made her appear, gillyflowers and pansies perpetually blooming on her stomacher. In 1602, a year before her death, the poet John Davies was gallantly insisting

> Time's young hours attend her still
> And her eyes and cheeks do fill
> With fresh youth and beauty

And the odd thing was that, despite the garish wig and the blackened teeth and the withered breasts (uncovered to the end as befitted a virgin), foreigners like the Venetian Ambassador Scarinelli, who saw her with pearls like pears roped about her brow, did indeed think that Elizabeth's beauty 'though past' has not entirely faded. And the German Thomas Platter swore he had seen the mask of a young woman 'no more than twenty years of age'. (Schama, 2001: 332)

The current shift in the relative ages of the population, with the elderly becoming far more numerous than the young, presents a challenge to find new, positive images of age with which to encourage the majority. The advances in medicine have taken some of the negative assumptions out of growing old. It need no longer be synonymous with a time of ill-health and as that threat lessens new opportunities open out. A person in their eighties should not automatically be assumed to be fragile, unsuitable for an overseas holiday as once might have been the case.

Medical statistics for Scottish general practice show that patients between the ages of 65 and 74 are likely to see their doctor about four times a year. Over 75 this rises to around five times. The three most common complaints which take them for a consultation are chest infections, depression and high blood-pressure. In enlightened practices much of the consultation will be to do with preventative medicine checking worrying symptoms to avoid major crises. The watch on hypertension is, for instance, related to the danger of a stroke and appropriate medication can reduce the risk to the patient and potential cost to the health-service budget.

Such perceptions have an important part to play in redressing the dread of age, yet realistically it is also a time of diminishment, and to the anxious can feel like a foretaste of dying. Limbs move more slowly, hearing and eyesight begin to fail. Aches and pains chart the advance of the increasing years. There is less energy to devote to the various tasks of living; we become impatient where once we might have taken time to sort out a problem or build a relationship.

If this description is accepted as reflecting a widespread emotional reaction, then it follows that there is much to be learned from those who have worked with other forms of loss and bereavement. Their insights can usefully be translated to apply to retirement and ageing, so that the final mood is not a backward-looking regret but a readiness to move to a new orientation. For example, William Worden in his book *Grief Counselling and Grief Therapy* (Worden, 1991) identifies four tasks in mourning. He uses the idea of 'task', rather than 'phases' advisedly to indicate that grief invites the mourner to address a piece of work, to take action and do something and not wait passively for a stage to pass. This, he argues, is more in keeping with Freud's concept of grief work.

This certainly applies in the handling of old age. Its progress requires an active response from the person who is growing old. It is not a time for passivity and acceptance but rather is to be greeted as a new stage of learning and adaptation. Worden lists the tasks of mourning related to the death of a person:

1. To accept the reality of the loss
2. To work through to the pain of grief
3. To adjust to an environment in which the deceased is missing
4. To relocate the deceased emotionally and move on with life

If we redefine these tasks in the context of old age, the loss with which we have to grapple is not the death of a significant other but of abilities and behaviour enjoyed in a previous phase of our own psychological reality. The alternative is to accept the changes and come to terms with them. It is part of ourselves that has died. It is in this context that the grief work has to be undertaken.

First, the reality of the loss needs to be accepted. Everyone who has worked with the bereaved knows the ways in which it is possible to avoid facing the painful truth of the death that has occurred. The same is the case with ageing. Denial takes a great many forms. Old people may dress and act in ways inappropriate to their age and avoid admitting the signs of increasing disability. Other mechanisms for denial include the accusation that 'Young people these days don't speak up, they mumble' which puts the blame for deafness on others; complaints about the quality of the lighting avoid accepting the fact of failing eyesight.

The accusation of crabbiness associated with old age comes from the tendency to put blame on to others to avoid self-criticism; but how often is this a mechanism for avoiding the truth of failing powers? Another symptom is that old people, rather than admit weakness will push themselves and perhaps their tired, ageing dogs to walk further than is beneficial, in order to prove their fitness. Breathlessness on the hills is disguised rather than accepted. Memory lapses are not only a source of irritation, they are disguised by jokes, and references to them by others are felt to be in bad taste. They carry disturbing implications that are feared in case they are the first signs of the onset of dementia. They are therefore also covered up.

In *Alice in Wonderland*, Lewis Carroll introduces a criticism of the representative pensioner who refuses to behave in a way appropriate to his age.

> You are old, Father William, the young man said
> And your hair has become very white;
> And yet you incessantly stand on your head –
> Do you think at your age it is right?

In contemporary culture advertisers would try to sell Father William the kind of long-lasting hair dye which would disguise grey flecks as they appeared on his head well before they had a chance to turn white. They would ignore his acrobatic exuberance, or perhaps applaud it as being consonant with his disguised appearance. This is a response directly opposed to Worden's prescription for the second task, 'to work through to the pain of grief'. It hurts to admit that the energy or the stamina that were once there have gone. The reason for the behaviour that aims at denial may lie in an attempt to avoid this second task. Yet if it is neglected, it is judged that the pain 'will manifest itself through some symptoms or other forms of aberrant behaviour'. This long-term warning is often neglected and the results may be either the projection of blame on to those around, damaging family and social relations, or else destructive behaviour like alcoholism. However the pressure to avoid the pain may not come from the individual alone. Worden comments:

> There may be a subtle interplay between society and the mourner which makes the completion of Task II more difficult. Society may be uncomfortable with the mourner's feelings and hence gives the implied message, 'You don't need to grieve, you are only feeling sorry for yourself'. Geoffrey Gorer recognises this and says 'Giving way to grief is stigmatised as morbid, unhealthy, demoralising. The proper action of a friend and well-wisher is felt to be distraction of a mourner from his or her grief'. (Worden, 1991: 13)

If this is true in the case of a reaction to death, it is even more important to recognize that it is likely to happen when a person is facing the emotional strains of handling old age. The pressure from the surrounding company is enhanced when the old are either their contemporaries or the selves whom they foresee they will become. Hence the collusion to avoid acknowledging that it is difficult to cope and to disguise the apparently unattractive image of being old. White hair or baldness are targets for advertisers offering a disguise or a cure. Cosmetics in general play on the fear of the physical signs of ageing. The television screens are full of promises that one brand of cream or another will defeat the wrinkles, keep skin youthful and hold age at bay. 'Don't deny your age, Defy it!' is one slogan which suggests that Lewis Carroll is a more mature counsellor in his colloquy with Father William than the cosmetic firms would be!

Worden's third task is 'To adjust to an environment in which the deceased is missing'. In terms of old age this is to live in tune with the physical and mental limitations that one's condition imposes. This may sound defeatist; resignation to a place on the shelf. That is only the case if old age is defined exclusively in terms of loss. The purpose of the grief work is to liberate the mourner from the trap of the past so that a new phase can be begun. This is Worden's final task, 'To relocate the deceased emotionally and move on with life'. In terms of the older person this is to abandon the regrets that will attend them if they live as a prisoner of the past and instead to encourage them to accept that the present offers new opportunities which can be no less fulfilling.

Previous experience will determine the attitudes that are brought to the handling of old age. I was a diocesan bishop for over a quarter of a century and during that period I was involved with a great many clergy as they were appointed to and resigned from the parishes they served. It became increasingly clear that the way in which they said their Hellos and Goodbyes was a measure of what they felt that they had achieved in their previous ministry and what they had to offer in the future.

I came to understand this behaviour by analogy with some of the animals that Christopher Robin owned in the books of A. A. Milne. As well as his bear Winnie the Pooh there was the depressed, morose donkey Eeyore and the bouncy character of Tigger whose most obvious characteristic was that when he said 'Hello!', you got sand in your ears. Not surprisingly the other animals agreed that he needed to be reformed and in *The House at Pooh Corner* there is a chapter in which Tigger is un-bounced. There have been clergy who, in similar mode, advanced on a new parish invincibly confident that their gifts were exactly what the congregation needed, even if this came as a surprise to the recipients and was not substantiated by evidence of past ministry by the clergy concerned. Sadly also there were characters who looked back with regret at their failures and mulled over them like Eeyore at his birthday party when the other animals brought presents that had got damaged in transit. He tried to make the best of them putting the burst balloon in and out of a honey jar that Pooh had emptied on the way. The clergy who left a job with a sense of grievance that their gifts were under-valued or that misunderstandings had arisen which prevented a

— 21 —

satisfactory expression of their vocation, presented a similar picture. Such people were never able wholly to detach themselves and move on; they always wanted to put things right to reduce their guilt or restore their self-esteem. The emotionally unfinished business drew them back, half in self-justification and half in expiation. I could see them stuck for ever with the burst balloon and the empty honey jar.

In both these situations there is a parallel with the process of retirement and ageing. Those who have a sense of fulfilment in life and are without too many regrets can let go with serenity, confident that their successors will appreciate the quality of the heritage they left behind and that between the generations there will be gratitude and not recrimination. They are the people who look forward to whatever may be next. Nevertheless if they do this without leaving proper space for regret and mourning they slip into denial and begin to share some of Tigger's insensitivity that prevents them from looking back and savouring the accomplishments of the past. The unfulfilled and disappointed go over the past and are unable to let it go.

What is needed is the double recognition that in both going and coming, not only from a job but from life itself, there is a proper mixture of sorrow and expectation, of tears and bounce. The practical question is, how does a person integrate the two conflicting emotions? In Worden's terms how can the experience of loss be contained, so that a new context for living is evolved? This must include the confidence to let go of the skills or stamina of the earlier phase and to move on to the positive task of reinvesting the emotional energy in a new context. This is especially relevant in examining the process of learning and development in old age, because, as has been suggested, the primary association with that stage is loss and diminishment and not growth at an intellectual or emotional level. Yet without that positive sense of contributing to the community and being a participant in life, old age would become a kind of waiting-room for death rather than a phase of living to which one can look forward.

This is not a new dilemma, although recent generations have

found fresh categories in which to describe it. Three thousand years ago, the Psalms used the language of religion to address the paradox of simultaneous diminishment and growth in old age:

> Those who are planted in the house of the Lord:
> shall flourish in the courts of our God.
> They shall still bear fruit in old age;
> they shall be green and succulent. (Psalm 92.12, 13)

Some further non-scriptural lines fill out the picture:

> I've seen withered roots, clawing on to life
> in soured soil;
> spindly branches, brittle with frustration,
> ready to crackle when anger strikes.
> This is the desert of the unfertile intelligence,
> swept by the bitter music of the piper
> for whom nobody danced.
> Half liberator, jackal Death
> waits to crunch the carcass, dried to an untimely end
> by disappointment.
>
> Jewels of fruit glisten in other trees
> that tap into deep reservoirs of being.
> Watered by affection they blossom
> in the spring time of maturity.
> At home in the delight of God
> they express the green glory of creation;
> to the last the sap rises
> and laughter stirs in the supple leaves.
>
> (Hare Duke, 1994)

It is clearly desirable to resolve the paradoxical task of staying 'green and succulent' in the brittleness of old age. But does this require more than resolving the tensions of mourning lost energies, position and competence? As well as letting go of the past we have a problem about where we will relocate its emotions and move on with life if the next stop is seen as the final one, at the crematorium. Irvin Yalom, Professor of Psychiatry at

Stanford University of Medicine, USA, has set out succinctly the dimensions of the problem:

> At one's core there is an ever-present conflict between the wish to continue to exist and the awareness of inevitable death . . . We know about death, intellectually we know the facts but we, that is the unconscious portion of the mind that protects us from overwhelming anxiety – have split off or dissociated, the terror associated with death. This dissociative process is unconscious, invisible to us, but we can be convinced of its existence in those rare episodes when the machinery of denial fails and death anxiety breaks through in full force . . . Most of us, most of the time live comfortably by uneasily avoiding the glance of death, by chuckling and agreeing with Woody Allen when he says 'I'm not afraid of death. I just don't want to be there when it happens'. But there is another way, a long tradition, that teaches us that full awareness of death ripens our wisdom and enriches our life.
> (Yalom, 1991: 5–7)

This involves both a short- and a long-term approach. First there is the immediate task of finding a new role when we are displaced by retirement from the position we have achieved. At the end of our working life we have to accept that we are no longer the wage-earners or the decision-makers. There is an agenda that is now closed, we have done what we could to make our mark. But that does not mean that we must withdraw from society. The need is then to find out what we can give and the appropriate way of making the contribution. Within the family it may be as a grandparent, within professional life as a consultant, within the community as a volunteer. On every hand there is an awareness that the older person has something that is too valuable to be lost. The difference between this and working life is that each individual must be free to offer the gift, it must not be demanded as of right. The assumption that grandparents are automatically child-minders or baby-sitters can sour family relationships. The gifts of age must not be mistaken for the rights of the next generation, nor the identity of the elders be confused on the twilight frontier. Clarity and open negotiation need to be the marks of family life. In this way the enjoyment that old age should provide will be safeguarded and the aim achieved of moving into another stage which replaces the satisfaction of the earlier one.

There is the danger that just at the point when people should be ready to let go, they hear a call to reinvent themselves. They do not have the luxury of coasting along in the style that they have learned over forty or fifty years of working life. Instead they are tempted to use what they have learned as a springboard into a new mode of contribution that can seem hostile. For instance, a solicitor, an architect or a parish priest may have found it attractive to retire sufficiently close to a former sphere of work to remain in contact with previous clients or parishioners. From that position the retired person may be sucked in to hear all their complaints about the new management and collude with their discontent. The former practitioner has all the knowledge to review each situation and to say what he or she would have done. There is an alternative. The professional imagination could hear the story, appreciate the choices which had to be made and offer not criticism of the newcomer but an explanation of how the decisions came to be made. The one is recognized as a supportive colleague, the other vilified as an interfering old busybody. The path an individual takes will depend on the confidence that he or she can place on the value of the past performance. This will in its turn determine whether retirement becomes an opportunity to make amends for a sense of failure or a celebration of a job well done. What sort of baggage are we carrying as we approach the twilit frontier? Nobody will be without a measure of guilt and dissatisfaction, but can they settle for a verdict which acquits them as 'good enough', rather than tormenting themselves with a demand that they shall hold on to the duty to make reparation until all outstanding accounts, as they conceive them, have been paid?

This is an issue that affects the mental health of many retired persons and their successors. To address this piece of adult learning is part of the spiritual growth to which everyone can aspire. Two paths lead to the same outcome. For some the self-exploration begins with a reflection on childhood and the way that family expectations or the cultural surroundings into which one was born influenced one's view of oneself. This largely relies on the insights of individual or social psychology. What did the behaviour of father or mother teach us? What impact did our school, our neighbourhood, our family or friends have on us? Having asked the questions it is possible to reflect what we want to do about it, affirming, rejecting or modifying it by conscious choice. For others there is a way of personal reflection, enquiring of oneself what the contemporary pattern of one's individual behaviour reveals. At the end of the day, a review of the choices made will show a person what he or she really values, as opposed to the alleged priorities. With this self-knowledge the door is open for change, although the choice may be neither easy nor obvious.

Part of the ambivalence about old age with which this chapter started is grounded in the sense of impotence with which it confronts us. So many abilities are taken from us by the advancing years. What is left is the power to reflect and to change internally. Confronted with an aspect of ourselves that we dislike we do not have to shrug our shoulders and accept it. There is time and opportunity for introspection and learning. We do not have to put up with our grumpy old personality, nor expect our families to do the same. We can confront the disappointed child who hides within us and do something about the pattern of resentment we have carried for years. Alternatively the compulsively altruistic 'servants' can reflect about what they have inflicted on their families as they have striven to deny themselves and always put others first. Perhaps they can begin to laugh at themselves and begin to make amends to their long-suffering spouses. This a vice to which the clergy are particularly addicted but it also infects many of the other helping professions as well. With such reflection there is a possibility of rich growth, as less full diaries release people to learn more about being human before others have to write their obituaries or they move on to a more rigorous assessment in another world.

At the same time we have recognized that this is a difficult, perhaps even a dangerous area, a twilit frontier and we need to ask who can accompany us. The traditional religious answer is 'God'. There is a ready-made quote from the Twenty-third Psalm:

> Yea, though I walk through the valley of the
>   shadow of death, I will fear no evil
> For thou art with me, thy rod and thy staff
>   comfort me. (v. 4)

But what grounds has the elderly person got for trusting this reassurance? If all his life long he has lived without any recognition of God, why now in a moment of uncertainty will it pay any dividends? The alternative is to look for a fellow human being who can stand by one. Once again there is an uncertainty about finding a person to fulfil that role. An adult surrounded by insecurity can all too easily regress to the fantasies of childhood and become either over-dependent or full of suspicion and mistrust. This is not an easy time to build up a secure relationship. In fact there is considerable case material to suggest that older people may quickly become victims of abuse by carers or family members who seek to exercise power over them in a number of ways, some by physical abuse, others by psychological or emotional manipulation, others by misusing whatever wealth they have (Pritchard, 1999).

It is tragically true that in the uncertainty of the final frontier, human relationships break down. The civilized boundaries between the generations are dissolved, parent and child roles are reversed and old animosities or patterns of violence re-emerge. Spiritual care in old age needs to include counselling for emotional adjustment, re-education and reflection on family life. Some of these topics will be touched on later in Chapters 7 and 8 where we examine the contribution of religious bodies, while recognizing that this issue is complicated in a secular age because it is not only those with religious beliefs who have spiritual needs. Nevertheless there is a tendency to feel that this should be the sphere of the priest, minister or religious representative. Yet the person who is most often in touch with the situation may well be the social worker who is involved with the assessment of a client's needs – medical, social, financial and emotional. However, Phyllida Parsloe, Emeritus Professor of Social Work in the University of Bristol, writes:

> One might argue that social workers should be able to help their clients to talk about spiritual needs and help them to find ways to meet them ... but my experience of social workers is that at least once they are trained, they seldom raise spiritual questions and I suspect that they sometimes make it difficult for clients to raise them.
>
> The State social services are still to an extent running away from their religious past. One of the strands from which present-day social services developed was the religious voluntary societies of the late nineteenth century. These societies were often engaged in evangelical activities as well as social services. Social workers today are at pains to reject this part of their history. In doing so they confuse spirituality, religion and evangelism and to be one the safe side avoid all three. (Parsloe, 1999)

It is not necessary to seek for fresh agencies to supply this deficiency but, instead, for all concerned to ensure that those already in contact with old people are equipped to handle such issues with confidence. The taboo surrounding the subject of death, and the inability to see it as the natural exit from living, skew the discussions about funeral arrangements, the decisions for a dignified death and many other practical issues to which we will return.

3

Changing the Climate

The retirement years can be full of new discoveries, but the experience of diminishment that was described in the last chapter brings also a flavour of dying. Old age involves letting go of both the role that we have built up in the outer world and the inner picture that sustained us. In consequence the four tasks involves in the mourning process were listed, suggesting that the same course needs to be followed in old age if we are to move from a sense of loss to an expectation of new life.

We explored the pain entailed in saying 'goodbye' to what is lost as we grow older. The purpose of this was not to open the doors to depression but to suggest a way to move to a new stage with a positive expectation. We need to find a fresh perspective on old age, not by denying the loss but by enjoying its compensations and the changed possibilities that it offers. Such a shift needs a revision of the generally held images. They assume that human life is parallel to the natural round of the seasons; childhood equates with spring and leads through summer and autumn to death in winter. This cycle is illustrated in the imagery of Robert Burns writing of his old friend John Anderson.

> John Anderson, my jo, John
> When we were first acquent;
> Your locks were like the raven,
> Your bony brow was brent;
> But now your brow is beld, John
> Your locks are like the snaw
> But blessing on your frosty pow
> John Anderson my jo.

If we accept the model of the year's cycle to describe a human life, we need to discover that there is more to the image of winter than the snowy hair that has replaced the raven locks and the hint that life, like the old year, is coming to an end. The cold weather brings gifts as well as loss. One example might be the beauty of the frozen patterns in the ice. In spring and summer the water in the river rushes on, you glimpse it and it is gone. In winter it is caught and held by the frost. The frenzy of the river in spate is slowed to make a pattern for the eye to contemplate and savour. Old age can be a time to pause and enjoy aspects of the natural world that had remained hidden in the business of active life. It can give time to watch the birds in one's neighbourhood, to pause and talk to a cat that in an earlier phase of life would have been ignored as one hurried to the train.

In a similar way there is an opportunity to relish the store of memories that can fill out a reflective evening by the fire. When one was young, life seemed to rush past at a breakneck speed, leaving little time to pause and reflect. Now, in retirement, a coherent pattern begins to emerge, woven into a unique design that is all one's own. Held in reflection, the years combine to form a total picture where the light and shade make a contrasting whole. Winter can suggest a welcome model for a ripe, contemplative old age.

Old age is sometimes described as 'life past its sell-by date'. But this again is to fall into the trap of seeing value at only one point of a life cycle. A hollow tree in the forest may be assumed to be no good because it is past its prime. The negative description focuses on the partly rotted trunk, the loose bark and the old dead branches which need to be cut out. But too little is made of the contribution of the hollow tree to the life of the woodland. It is easily written off as having no future. The inner core may have fallen victim to disease and rotted away but it is still a focus of life. Its outer bark will have thickened with age and its roots will have penetrated deeper into the soil. This will give it a stability against the winter gales. Younger trees are bent under the wind pressure caught by their heavy foliage, like a ship with too great a weight of sail, and are in danger of blowing over. The hollow tree stands firm in the ground and offers less resistance to the gale, and so becomes a secure home to a host of woodland creatures. Insects live under the bark, birds can burrow into the soft wood to find a useful site for a nest and small mammals make a home in its roots.

This image is a reminder not to write off old age. It can be a time that finds a person more firmly fixed in place, able to resist the squalls of hostile opinion or disapproval that shake the young. Because the elderly have less to prove, they are more available to offer shelter to unlikely people or strange ideas. Their hospitality can be more generous, not seeking a return of thanks or credit, just enjoying the fun of exploring new friends or fresh ideas.

In another analogy, like the carpet of snow that nurtures the crocuses, grandparents can offer time and interest to their grandchildren when parents are too preoccupied. The next spring depends on the gifts of the winter, it is not simply a matter of replacing an unfavourable season with another which fosters growth. Each has its own part to play that complements the other.

All these are positive images of age and its gifts, but how do they take root in the view of society or in the self-perception of senior citizens who can easily identify with the low esteem which they are accorded? At times older people have allowed themselves to collude in the denigration of their generation. 'We are past it,' they say. The prevailing attitude is reinforced by both sides, young and old. This in its turn becomes the seed-bed from which elder abuse derives because the older person is felt to be in the way or offering a contradictory model to the grandchildren. There follows verbal abuse, criticizing what they have to offer or even emotional abuse which denies them access to the younger children because their ideas are felt to be obstructive. A healthy society will have a view of its elders which makes it impossible to be antagonistic or to exploit them.

Sometimes a rosy picture is painted of other cultures in which the elders are honoured. There is for instance a view that within Hindu culture there is a reverence for older people. These are defined as those who have moved through at least the first three of the four stages of life which begin in childhood with the way of 'the student', then 'the householder', 'the forest dweller' and finally progress to the total renunciation of the world which is the highest spiritual state of all, 'the sage'. With such a scheme the maturity of a person is expected to develop in parallel with his or her advancing years. The one is assumed to imply the other. As the circumstances of old age have changed this is no longer the case. The difference was demonstrated at a seminar in Edinburgh at which a consultant geriatrician from India spoke. He described the traditional expectations of the spiritual path, but went on to give case material from his own practice where he met with patients suffering from Alzheimer's disease.

One old lady was brought from an old people's home because she was suffering from the delusion that she had been robbed. The facts were that the warden of the home had explained to her as a new resident that all jewellery would be kept in the office safe. So the rings and brooches that she usually wore were stored there. She forgot this and began her accusations. When she was brought to the doctor she began the story of her imagined loss and, as part of the description, pulled at her sari to demonstrate that the jewellery was not about her person. The attendant began to slap her to stop her as though she were a naughty child. The theory of respect for the old had been formulated in a time when senile dementia was unknown, probably because too few survived to suffer from it. There can now be no automatic assumption in any culture that old people will be the revered repositories of wisdom.

This issue has been addressed in an American work *The Moral Challenge of Alzheimer Disease* by Professor Stephen Post. He foresees that as

> those aged 85 and older constitute the fastest-growing age group, the numbers of elderly persons with chronic dementing diseases will reach a level of magnitude that human history has never before witnessed. There is a potential for moral travesty or moral triumph. Because we have successfully eliminated many of the conditions that shorten the human life

span, the thickness and thinness (quality) of our moral respect for elderly and debilitated persons takes on a new importance. The demands of filial morality and communal regard for elderly persons set forth in virtually all traditional social thought are now higher. (Post, 1995)

This leads him to the question, 'Do we have the moral resources to navigate this crisis?' In itself this is part of the wider issue of how the status of older people is to be established and maintained at every level. Alzheimer's disease has become the dramatic short-hand for all the diminishments of age but from the moment of retirement there are smaller 'bereavements' to be handled, loss of status and identity, perhaps the motivation for the day has gone or one is deprived of companionship at the workplace.

Visual images dominate our communications. We need to look to the inspiration of the television dramatists to produce a more engaging picture of old age than the one that emerged from Victor Meldrew with *One Foot in the Grave*. Even the traffic signs that warn of old people crossing need some scrutiny; must the figures they portray be quite so bowed and decrepit? All the others who play a part in forming public opinion need to reflect on their contribution. Racism has been recognized as a corrosive influence in society; the same is true of the barrier that ageism erects. Every age group needs to be aware of it and to guard against it, but the elderly themselves have some responsibility in this matter and should be sensitive to the way in which they are portrayed or the impression that they themselves give. The subject of the pension has been over the years a political bone of contention. On the one hand it is only right that the older generation should share proportionately in the current wealth of the nation. Any fiscal policy which denies this possibility is an institutionalized form of the elder abuse to which reference has been made earlier. On the other hand it would be an unhappy demonstration of a deep-seated greed in our culture if the new and increasing political clout of the pensioners' vote were used to ensure them a disproportionate slice of the available financial cake. It is not unreasonable to hope that the elders should offer a model of maturity and selflessness to their children and grand-children. A campaign for justice in all sections of the community, single parents, the disabled, the homeless, as well as the elderly themselves, would challenge the whole community to consider its responsibilities. This approach by the old would have a positive resonance with the ideals of the Hindu schema. There it is expected that in the earlier stages of life, the householder, as he builds up a family will respond to the pressure to meet their needs. This will involve him in acquiring sufficient resources to house, clothe, feed and bring up his children. When this duty is fulfilled and the responsibility for his family is no longer on his shoulders, he is expected to move on to become the 'hermit' or 'forest dweller' and begin to reflect on how little material possessions bring contentment to the individual. Old age then becomes the period of letting go and accepting what is enough, not of strident campaigning for more. Yet this ideal attitude can only develop in those who feel that they have 'enough' and are not denied their basic rights. This sense that justice has been done will then make room for generosity and concern for the needs of others rather than one's own. In its turn, this experience will have the double benefit that it will build a better society world-wide and also give to older people the sense that they are contributing to the future.

With this however goes another dilemma for the old. How can they make their voices heard in shaping a society that they believe to be just? If they are not to feel marginalized and devalued, they need a place to share in the political and moral debates of the day. If instead they are relegated to the ghetto of the page reserved for 'Letters to the Editor' their discontent will grow and their consequent stridency will make them less credible. Dylan Thomas wrote a poem for his father the old schoolmaster with the title 'Do not go gentle into that good night'. In it he details all the frustrations of old age, its failures and disappointments, the reasons why it 'should burn and rave at close of day'. Among these he sees the angry impotence of the thinkers and philosophers:

> Though wise men at their end know dark is right,
> Because their words had forked no lightning they
> Do not go gentle into that good night.

As he imagined it, these were the men who had seen what needed doing, but nobody had listened. 'Their words had forked no lightning' in terms of political or social action. They shared the curse of the prophetess Cassandra, always to be right and never believed. It is one of the hardest deprivations of retirement to be on the side-lines of decision-making, relegated from the Cabinet, the Board Room, the parish, the surgery or perhaps even the family conference. It feels as though a life-time's skills or experience are being ignored. How does the pattern of the mourning process apply in these circumstances? Can the retired realistically seek to move from the pain of acknowledged loss to a positive new mode of participation?

In Europe that has been much talk of 'active citizenship' for the older generation and a series of congresses known as Euroforums have met in Baden-Württemberg, Bialystok (Poland), Catalonia and Scotland to address this largely as a political issue. These have resulted in the establishment of a Eurolink Age desk in Brussels. This is concerned with mobilizing communicaton within Europe and at the same time making it clear that the notion of citizenship must include not only participation but the other criteria set out in the conclusions of the Year of The Older Person, independence, care, self-fulfilment and dignity. To achieve them the political will must be found to fund long-term care, life-long learning and appropriate housing. This still leaves the personal and spiritual agenda unaddressed. In particular at the end of these practical programmes there remains the inescapable necessity of confronting and handling the process of dying. Part of the reality of this is that as a society we need to be prepared to take legal, financial and emotional decisions that take into account the current state of scientific advance, changed religious beliefs and attitudes towards dying. Practical details will be discussed in Chapter 9, but meanwhile it needs to be noted that as long as this nettle remains ungrasped and death is not faced we will remain more like children afraid of the dark than adult human beings confidently preparing for the journey that we know must be made.

Individuals will not have a coherent image of death until they have come to terms with the bereavement of old age. The moment of death is not an isolated end intervening starkly and unannounced. It comes most naturally at the end of a process of ageing, even though there is a truth in the comment that Heidegger attributes to the 'Bohemian ploughman', 'As soon as a man comes to life, he is at once old enough to die' (Heidegger, 1967: 289). However strenuously we seek to avoid it, as human beings we know that we will one day die and our lives need to take account of this truth. It can be argued that this understanding contributes not simply to the well-being of the individual but to the whole of society. In his magisterial study *Childhood and Society*, Erikson wrote 'Healthy children will not fear life if their elders have integrity enough not to fear death' (Erikson, 1965: 261). The realism of grandparents who have come to terms with their mortality will contribute to a wholesome world.

The attitude which is adapted to the journey, balancing loss and expectation, is most helpfully summed up in the poetry of the Psalms. The author of Psalm 119 writes: 'I am become like a bottle in the smoke' (v. 83). The picture will not be immediately understood until it is recognized that in the world which he is describing, wine was stored in a goatskin 'bottle' that hung by the kitchen fire. The image then emerges of the unattractive, gnarled wineskin blackened by smoke that nevertheless contains a vintage brew slowly maturing. It has nothing to show on the outside but the quality is within. This is an analogy which is immediately understandable in Scotland in relation to malt whisky where age determines both taste and price!

This matches the feelings that the psalmist has of his own worth. Externally he can say, 'I am small, of little account'. Internally it is a different case: 'Trouble and distress had come upon me, yet your commandments are my delight' (vv. 141 and 143). From this inner evaluation he finds his reassurance:

Your commandment has made me wiser than my enemies
and it is always with me.
I have more understanding than all my teachers,
for your decrees are my study. (vv. 98, 99)

The image of 'the bottle in the smoke' is therefore realistic and reassuring. It reflects the value that the writer puts on himself, deriving from his inner life. Whatever is happening in the external world, the individual has managed to hold on to the sense of the vintage wine within.

This is not merely a prescription for a desirable psychological state. It is a development that can be observed within a personality. Even when the context of a life seems to have deteriorated, there can be a determination within a person to hold on to and affirm his or her inner life. From a person's unconscious mind dreams can come which are concerned to counterbalance the perceived losses of day-to-day living.

This was illustrated by a 96-year-old whom I was visiting in an old people's home. She was distressed by the external circumstances of her day-to-day living. She was not convinced that life still had anything to offer or that she had any contribution to make. 'I can't think why I have been left,' she complained as she fretted about the inconvenience of her living arrangements, and struggled with her increasing blindness and isolation. Then one afternoon she described a dream in which she had met an old man on a mountain path and she was convinced that his name was Melchizedek. She was not sure that she knew who such a character was, but given her church background in childhood it was safe to guess that this shadowy figure from the Old Testament had a meaning that was embedded somewhere in her unconscious memories. A reference to the Book of Genesis reminded her of the legend of Abraham's return after a victorious battle when he was met by various local potentates. The account ends 'Melchizedek, king of Salem, brought forth bread and wine and he was the priest of the most high God. And he blessed him' (Genesis 14. 18). Christian theology which she had probably heard quoted, but only retained in unconscious memory, has amplified the story to see a reference to the bread and wine of Communion foretold in the Old Testament. Meanwhile Melchizedek reappears in the Letter to the Hebrews, to provide a tortuous argument about the significance of Christ, but attached to him at that point is a slogan that has echoed all through debates about Christian ministry, 'a priest for ever after the order of Melchizedek'.

We stumbled through this maze as best we could, patching together childhood memories of Bible stories and the inner significance of the dream which she felt was important. It seemed that she was reaffirming the inner sense of wisdom that she had come to know in herself and which her friends recognized, but which had perhaps been diminished by her recent experiences until she had begun to feel that she was 'just a silly old woman'. Here was the icon of Melchizedek to reassure her that the strength of her inner self, her wisdom, remained as part of her core being. Perhaps this is a perception that all old people need to share as the way into the reinvestment of their energies in a new way forward. The result of our conversation was the joint composition of the poem that follows:

> The grey dawn catches colour in God's light,
> Lost stories, fanned from ash and ember glow.
> Dimmed eyes, retrained to focus inner sight
> Discern old tales forgotten long ago.
>
> Cobwebbed in mystery, both King and Priest,
> Melchizedek appears with bread and wine,
> Bearing for Abraham a victory feast,
> First showing of Christ's eucharistic sign.
>
> Crowned with the names of Justice and of Peace,
> He shadowed forth the King who'd come to give
> His life's obedience for the world's release
> And in his death ensure that we might live.
>
> Melchizedek betokens all our race,
> Like him, reflecting glory from God's face,
> We learn to chart the uncertain future's course

By wisdom gathered from life's ancient source.
Patience must hold until we've told our tale
Then with the west-bound breezes we'll set sail.

'That's good,' she said, 'we must make it part of my funeral service.' That was the way it was a year or so later.

An account of a more sustained undertaking came from an elderly widow who moved away from the neighbourhood where friends still lived, to be with her daughter and family some 50 miles away. She had considered the danger of loneliness, because her daughter was out at work much of the day. Arrived at her new home, she began to feel isolated from the spiritual conversations that she had enjoyed with her friends. As a first move to re-establish the ambience that she was missing, she placed in the shop window of a local newsagent a postcard which read: 'Elderly lady with an interest in Angels would like to meet another similarly minded.' This produced no replies but she was not dismayed. Instead she undertook a review of her life, its gifts and achievements. For this she used a format that her daughter had acquired at a workshop designed to encourage older people 'to revitalize their positivity and creativity around the future'.

The introduction to the workshop proposes an activity to help clarify what the members want out of life. The task begins with compiling a list of 'My Abilities'. The instructions for this are: 'Without thinking too deeply, write down as fast as you can every positive quality, ability, attribute, skill that you have. Write down nothing negative. If you are good at something that you hate doing, don't write it down.' Examples offered are: 'I can type, play the piano a bit, work a word-processor, grow flowers and vegetables. I can cook, choose colour schemes, decorate, be good company, organize hassle-free holidays, I can listen to my friends' problems, I am a good letter writer.' If this is done in the context of a workshop, the instructions go on: 'When you start running out of ideas, share your lists with the people in your group and try to add one or two more ideas.'

On a new sheet of paper the members are next invited to

list the roles that they undertake. Again the instructions are: 'Without thinking too deeply, write down as fast as you can every role you play in your life.' Examples are: 'mother, daughter, neighbour, friend, teacher, listener, gardener, organizer'.

The third list is made up of 'Things I want to create'. Once again the choice is wide, with examples ranging from 'a garden, a peaceful room, a poem' to 'a way to feel more whole, peace, laughter, excitement, opportunities to have fun, a bigger circle of friends'.

For a final stage the instructions read: 'Go back over your three lists and, one at a time, choose the three most important thing from each list. You can cheat if you want, and put things together. Juggle around with your words so that they make sense together, i.e the attributes and roles do actually relate to the aspirations.' Since my friend was on her own, she set about the exercise in private. The result of her inner audit, outlining how she wanted to spend the rest of her days read as follows:

My purpose over the coming time is to use
my realization that I am a child of God and thus
    capable of anything,
my positive attitude to my deafness and other disabilities
and my higher consciousness . . .
Through my roles as
Guardian and elder within my family whose newest
    and most precious member is little Soli,
Creative homemaker,
Plant tender and guardian of nature,
Source of harmony between people.
In order to create
A gentle pathway from this life into the next by
    adapting to new spiritual manifestations,
A beautiful and harmonious experience of ageing
A contribution to the healing of our planet by helping to
make a habitat for plants and wildlife.

She died some months after completing the exercise so there was no opportunity for her to undertake a subsequent review, but her family were so delighted by her determination to meet her last stage of life with a forward-looking enthusiasm that they printed her resolution on the service sheet for her funeral. She too, they felt, had taken a personal stand against the dark, negative side of old age, which they wanted to celebrate and hand on to others as part of an attempt to change the climate of opinion.

4

Permission to Play

Adult life, as most people experience it, is largely concerned with tasks to be done. We are defined by our job or our career. 'What do you do?' people ask, and as we tell them we acquire an identity. When we are children it is accepted that we should play but even behind the games, at least for the adults watching, lies the question: 'What is he going to be when he grows up?'

Once we have started an adult working life, we complain that there are not enough hours in the day. Time is 'the enemy' which defeats our endeavours to complete a task. In retirement work has been put behind. Nobody else schedules the day, it is mine to fill as I choose. As long as the daylight lasts there is time for doing the garden or walking the dog. There should be time for friends and time for writing letters, time for reflection and time for hobbies. The promise that such a pattern offers is space, the opportunity to savour, to reflect, to enjoy and perhaps make new discoveries at one's leisure. Yet the experience of retirement often fails to match this idyllic picture. For some the unstructured time becomes an accuser who has to be 'killed'. Others fear the invasion of those who threaten to take them over because there is no diary with which to defend the day against them. 'I'm sorry the afternoon is full' no longer trips off the tongue, and if it did it would no longer be believed. One is made both guilty and vulnerable by the blank space.

At a meeting of senior citizens I encountered my former bank manager. He confessed to me with embarrassment that since his wife's death he lived in an old people's home and found himself gazing all day at a television screen 'to pass the time'. He found nothing creative in the day's space, only vacuity and, since he was the product of the work ethic where time was money, he felt guilty at the waste. The hands of the clock were an accusation;

as they moved he did nothing and that felt bad. Others have a need to present the image of a bustling life, so they complain that they are busier than ever in retirement. 'Is that really true and, if so, is it fun?' I want to ask them. Are there painful feelings, like disappointment, to be kept at bay by the pretence or is there the compulsion to be doing because an empty diary is a symbol of powerlessness? Is there a fear that without the public façade of being in the swim of activity with everybody else, one's meaning and identity will begin to be eroded?

Such a disheartening response is bred by the view that a worthwhile life must be defined in terms of crude productivity. There are many roles to be undertaken in retirement as a volunteer which directly impact on the community, and to these we return later, but the first place should be given to enhancing the quality of the individual's own life, making room for growth, providing pleasure and enjoyment. If this is the case we need to take seriously the purpose and priority of play.

As I faced the prospect of retirement after a busy life as a diocesan bishop, I found that I needed to reaffirm for myself the value of play. This was expressed in one poem in a book published at that time.

> It takes a kind of courage
> to find time for play.
> Work is what's expected; sober thoughts,
> A misership of time hoarding the precious minutes.
> Fun yields no dividends,
> No bonuses for jokes.
> Work earns the wages;
> The jobless are devalued.
> Computer haunted
> we've got it wrong.
> Machines are made to whirr and turn
> Faultless, precise, achieving;
> The human spirit should have space to soar
> To wild absurdity.
> We need permission to uncage our poet.

Eyes that rest on beauty
Seem ineffectual compared to hands that hammer.
Yet the time I take off
From industrious striving
To watch, enjoy my friendships, delight in touch
   and taste
Nourishes my true self.

Thank God for the dreams
In which we mount our fiery imaginations
And ride off into the misty mountains.
Night takes to task the busy day;
But why am I ashamed to claim the right to
   conscious play
Within the waking world?

When I can sit and let my mind catch fire
I understand how God sang for fun
Calling, out of nothing, all creation.
Wagtails bounce and flip their feathers,
Salmon leap,
The world turns, the planets wheel,
Tiny or vast;
Orchestrated into a joyful tune,
They become the models of all making.

Dreams, imagination, and God's laughter in creation
Invite me out of my industrious solemnity
To take the task of playing seriously
Until my marred manhood
Is recreated in the child I have denied.

                                         (Hare Duke, 1994)

Old age gives us the opportunity to recover this lost dimension
of our humanity. With working life completed there is no task
to be pursued, no credit to be earned. As a result the pattern can
revert to the inclusion of play, not set apart in a special kind of
therapy but found in the reality of ordinary life. This, however,
is not to be seen as a way of filling in time, another device for

getting through the day. The play of childhood is not a stop-gap before proper academic learning takes place. In the same way the play of old age is not a waste of the months and years of retirement. At both phases of life, play is a serious means of engaging with the task of development; it is a genuine piece of work, although not in the manner of earning and exchange that defines most of adult working life. If we have been successful in that area we will probably want to carry the same sense of achievement into retirement. But might part of the change from working life be a release from such a pressure? There is a lesson to be learned from childhood and its play which has no immediate reward. It is an activity that needs no justification except that it is fun in its own right. Nevertheless it carries a hidden pay-off because it is an important part of a person's growth and a preparation for a new stage of living. This is the parallel that I want to explore.

D. W. Winnicott, a paediatrician who went on to become a child psychoanalyst, made a considerable study of children's play. He identified the less obvious purposes that lay behind their games. As he watched his young patients at play he came to realize that the teddy bears and the other toys that littered his consulting-room floor were much more than fun objects to provide pleasure and distraction. As children played with them, they became tools to master the anxieties which had brought his young patients to him because they could not be put into words. The games with dolls and teddy bears gave expression to feelings, ideas and impulses which were too frightening for the children to acknowledge as their own, in case they might get out of control. A little boy might find it impossible to express his rage with a parent but his teddy bear could be 'very cross' because the child did not have to admit that the anger under scrutiny really belonged to himself. Relationships with siblings can be stormy; in the inner, unconscious world a child may wish his younger brother or sister dead. Such murderous feelings have to be hidden because they feel so wicked but the forbidden fantasies can be played out safely with toys. When the unacceptable feelings can be acknowledged for what they are, the child is ready to move on to see the difference between fantasy and action and to find a balance between loving and hating the people who matter.

Within this theoretical framework Winnicott interpreted the particular form that play takes for any individual child, relating it to the anxiety felt as part of his or her experience. Toys became a way of managing the transition from the private inner world of the infant to real-life relationships with external people or 'objects' who are entirely outwith his control. They were the 'transitional objects' with which he could experiment, acknowledging his aggression or other difficult emotions without giving them a definite focus (Winnicott, 1964).

The process of growing up does not finish in childhood. Adult life still needs its transitional objects to provide bridges across other gaps. At this stage however, suggests Winnicott, the actual toys are replaced by fantasy and the use of art forms and religious practice. This is not to belittle religion but to understand to what area of psychic activity it belongs. Such thinking implies parallel processes of development in adult life and in childhood. The child uses play with toys to develop to the fully mature 'object relationships' of adult life. Within a religious framework the final relationship of the believer to God or ultimate reality is sought by whatever means a person's culture has provided. In the case of a Christian these will be the temporal intermediaries of the Church, the sacraments and the Bible. None of these are to be elevated to the status of the final object of worship. It would be equally as unsatisfactory for adults to grow up to marry their teddy bears as it is to attribute divine qualities to the 'toys' of religion. They have a vitally important part to play in sustaining a person through various stages of life, not least the anxieties of old age and the facing of mortality. Yet the Church's story past and present is full of devout believers separating themselves from doctrinal opponents who have disagreed with them over the Bible or sacraments. The energy that fuels the contests arises because they have failed to understand the status of the transitional objects. It is always a warning sign when the adjective 'Holy' is attached to a religious object or construct that has originated in the sphere of human organization or history. 'Holy' Church has been defended or promoted with violence either within the Christian community or in conflict with other world faiths. The same has been true of almost every religion. Swords have been drawn to defend shrines and relics; and theological constructs have been promoted by armies as well as clergy, guns as well as holy books. Because the toys have been given divine status they have become idols and, like idols they have taken on the vicious characteristics of human domination. Meanwhile, by virtue of their 'divinity', they have offered absolution for the inhuman behaviour of their devotees.

A further interpretation of the interaction between play and religious faith is to be found in the work of Peter Berger. A sociologist seeking to examine the structure of reality, Berger was led to find evidence for the supernatural in aspects of ordinary living that are often seen as unremarkable and taken for granted. In his book *A Rumour of Angels* he sets out his arguments. First, the practice of science depends on a reliable natural order so that experiments can be conducted with the confidence that in similar conditions a given series of actions will produce similar results. The pattern of reliability is evidence for an order which is something akin to 'the mind of God'. In the same way society needs to be able to depend upon a shared moral structure to give it a civilized cohesion. Thirdly, the continuance of human life is sustained by the universal ability to play, to hope and to laugh; a mother comforting her child in the night assures him 'It's all right'. This is not a desperate plea for the unwanted crying to be quieted, but a fundamental reassurance that all is well. All these observable phenomena which are woven into the fabric of our existence provide 'signals of transcendence', pointing toward a supernatural order that underlies and sustains daily living, hence his title *A Rumour of Angels*.

Play and the other 'signals' go beyond the obvious accountancy of material rewards and point to a value system in which we find our true selves by abandoning our status and becoming as little children. Play has a special relevance because it involves losing our adult persona or importance. This may mean laughing at ourselves or letting go of the need to be prized or rewarded.

We may risk trying our hand at painting or writing poetry; we may listen to music, or respond in dance, without having to justify the activities by external rewards. It is noticeable that the presence of children may give us permission to engage in the more extravagant expressions of play. Paper hats are more spontaneously donned at Christmas when children have pulled the crackers.

If the ability to play is one of the qualities more easily recovered in old age, then it may be that we can use it to persuade our adult children that laughter is a vital component in human living; and that the gift of play is a liberation from the pressure of seeking justification for all our undertakings in terms of measurable outcomes. The discovery of the Now, the ability to find significance in the immediate encounter, the scent of a flower or the song of a bird, has long been recognized in many world faiths as a mark of spiritual enlightenment, the gift of the realized person. We have already noted that the table of illnesses that take the elderly in Scotland to consult their doctor reveals that hypertension, depression and anxiety states were three of the top six complaints. This may indicate that there could be a hidden pay-off to play if it makes life more manageable.

Meanwhile on a broader canvas, Peter Berger finds another meaning for play in the overcoming of tragedy. As it ameliorates the natural reactions of fear and grief it becomes a powerful witness to a realm of being that goes beyond terrestrial or mundane experience. By way of explanation he cites an example:

Just before the Soviet troops occupied Vienna in 1945, the Vienna Philharmonic gave one of its scheduled concerts. There was fighting in the immediate proximity of the city and the concert goers could hear the rumbling of the guns in the distance. The entry of the Soviet army interrupted the concert schedule, if I am not mistaken, for about a week. Then the concerts resumed as scheduled. In the universe of that particular play the world shattering events of the Soviet invasion, the overthrow of one empire and the cataclysmic appearance of another, meant a small interruption in the programme. Was this simply a case of callousness or indifference to suffering? Perhaps in the case of some individuals, but, basically, I would say not. It was rather an affirmation of the ultimate triumph of all human gestures of creative beauty over the gestures of destruction, and even over the ugliness of war and death. (Berger, 1970: 78)

In the same way at the height of the ethnic violence in Bosnia in May 1992 there was an incident in which 22 people in a bread queue were killed in Sarajevo. One musician, Vedran Smajlovic, was so appalled by the carnage that he appeared for 22 days in Vaesmiskina Street, the scene of the massacre, with his cello, wearing his white tie and tails and played the Albinoni Adagio. It was half protest and half political statement about the cultural heritage of Bosnia-Herzegovina. 'This is part of Europe, it must not be abandoned.' That cello and its appeal were heard around the world. Musicians in Scotland made heroic efforts to rescue Vedran from personal danger as he took his protest to graveyards where he continued to play. They also took up his message to relay it to the West. Once again in the playing of music there was the rumour of angels, a window opened on to the transcendent world of love and the values of civilization. Those who know him are keen to avoid any sanctification of Vedran in this story. He was, they stress, a very human person, most chiefly distinguished by his ability to clown and with a deep dedication to the cause of music which he inherited from his father. Strands from his Muslim inheritance and his Catholic upbringing, a taste for life, a sense of justice and a determination to hold on to his convictions produced a player whose protest made a difference at one moment to the imagination of Europeans. His gift was not high morality or political genius, it was to play his cello. The message was much the same as that of the mother comforting her child. Her instinctive reassurance and the notes of the cello cannot claim any irrefutable logic. They come from the emotional seat of laughter, tears and play.

The importance of this is that it brings with it a flavour of the supernatural world, offering 'a signal of transcendence' at just the time when our natural sense suggests that we are letting go of the assurance of everyday experience. Old age has its own particular brand of anxiety as the elder, like the growing child, faces a new transition for which there are no precedents. As the infant leaves the womb for a totally unknown experience, so death is a tunnel into the undescribable. Does the transitional play of childhood offer some clue as to how this might be managed? Before it occurs, old age provides us with the space for a tranquil focus, sometimes on nature, the birds, the sunset, the garden, the sea or the countryside, sometimes on the delight of grandchildren or old friends, sometimes on a clear-eyed evaluation of the past.

For those who look to a continuance of life after death, the recovery of the attitude which enjoys activities in their own right and does not need to seek beyond the present delight, may have in it a hint of a new possibility. Even without reading into it a theological meaning, the music of the Vienna Philharmonic Orchestra and Sarajevo's cello had a power to lift their contemporaries above the immediate violence and barbarity, and to open a door of hope, just as the play of childhood took the infant out of the trap of the emotions that threatened to overwhelm her.

A contribution which might incidentally emerge from this re-evaluation could be in the role of the elders as representatives of a counter-culture, questioning the urgent ambition that once drove their generation and still holds their children in thrall. Is retirement the time to challenge the priority once given to achievement? With advancing years may come different understandings of integrity or loyalty in friendships and marriage. Historically, the First World War provides a parallel with our present situation. In its course, for some the realization dawned that the confrontation in which they were engaged had lost its meaning. Wilfred Owen epitomized the emotional confusion in his immortal phrase addressed to the dead German soldier as he imagined them both meeting in Hell: 'I am the enemy you killed, my friend.' He and Siegfried Sassoon are two of the best-known names who featured on the patient list of the psychiatric hospital at Craiglockhart in Edinburgh. That bit of history has been captured in the 'Regeneration trilogy' by Pat Barker, half novel, half documentary recording the work of the psychiatrist Dr Rivers and chronicling some of his despair as he helped soldiers to become psychologically stable enough to return to the insane slaughter. The paradox is summed up in the final chapter where Rivers struggles to interpret the unintelligible phrase of a former patient who has returned fatally wounded and from his shattered jaw is only able to articulate the cry 'Shotwafit'. The doctor eventually disentangles the message as 'it's not worth it' and realizes that his mental hospital has become the only place where the sane voice of humanity can be heard and understood as it confronts the madness of the established values of nationalism (Barker, 1966).

It is the task of historians to explain the crises or mistakes of humanity in relation to earlier events, so that history is not a series of random happenings but can be seen to have a meaning. For instance, the rise of Nazism needs to be understood as in part stemming from the punitive treatment meted out to Germany by the victorious Allies in the Treaty of Versailles (1919) which left a legacy of perceived injustice. This gave National Socialism a platform from which to seek popular support for their political programme. The logic of cause and effect helps remove the fantasy of demonic elements from the narrative and leaves room to learn from past mistakes. So too time taken in retirement to review one's personal history can contribute to our understanding of what was going on within the family or amongst friends to produce some of the clearly remembered results, bad as well as good. As a result, resentment or recrimination can then be replaced by insight that enables forgiveness. The clarity of hindsight can also help the individual come to terms with his or her own mistakes, leading to a greater gentleness in reflecting on the part that they and others played. The lessons emerging may also be shared to build a more hopeful and less disturbed future.

Yet how far are we prepared to allow ourselves such reflection? Age has liberated us from work; is there something more productive to which we should dedicate ourselves? We are unused to the luxury of time and space unless there is the sense of having 'earned' a holiday. Is it simply a waste of time to 'replay' the past or does the freedom from the discipline of work enrich life in a variety of ways that wait to be discovered?

Between childhood and retirement, games take on a serious social purpose. They appear on a CV; they are justified as building character, making significant social contacts or leading somewhere. In *Who's Who* the space allocated to 'hobbies' is often used by the persons composing their personal entry to make a statement about themselves, sometimes listing activities that do them credit or else becoming a kind of protest against prevailing attitudes. What then happens to us and our spare time after retirement? Can we abandon the habit of a lifetime and be content to live without the justification of meaningful activities; or perhaps discover a new value in what we once disregarded? The relative value of the games that appeal to the retired may be a matter of argument. The advocates of golf will stress the double benefit of exercise on the fairway and the company in the club house. Bingo, with probably a larger constituency, offers the same inducement of company together with the hope of lucky winnings.

A national survey was carried out in Scotland, primarily concerned with marketing, but in a section headed 'Hobbies and Activities' it listed all the possible 'leisure interests and activities' that might appeal. The interesting schedule included Book-reading, Bird-watching, Collecting, Cooking, Crosswords, DIY, Fishing, Football, Gardening, Golf, Grandchildren, Home computing, Knitting, Photography, Religious activities, Self-improvement, Sewing/needlework, Theatre/cultural art events, Wildlife/environment. Many of these options represent personal pleasure in acquiring skills or knowledge, others offer the reward of companionship, and finally there is the altruism of volunteering. Does that then require a worthwhile outcome to justify it? We may, for instance, look for a return from our volunteering in terms of gratitude or the enhancement of our civic status. How much time and energy is an individual prepared to give up for the sheer joy of involvement? The whole topic of volunteering will be treated later under the other aspect of it as part of Lifelong Learning (Chapter 5).

The question of what we do with our retirement, if handled one way will carry the dynamics of our working life with us. If our choices are determined by the mathematics of input and outcome, we will remain part of the community of earning and exchange which defines most adult living. This is likely to be subject to the same frustrations that attended our working lives. The politics of the golf club will share the same elements of power-seeking, jealousy, deception or bartering that characterized trade union, board room, party caucus or church committee.

We have seen how Peter Berger in *A Rumour of Angels* gave a special place to play as the activity which provides a way into a different set of values. His major example was drawn from warfare when the human situation becomes overwhelmingly tragic. The action of play can make a statement which does not deny the fear or horror of the immediate experience but gives expression to it in a more manageable medium. In the same way, if a person is facing a transition from a safe, well-explored experience of living to face instead either annihilation or the uncertainty of an unknown mode of being, it may be that experimenting with some new technique for finding inner stillness will provide a resource. The Sufi, the Buddhist and the Christian all have common insights which emerge from a spiritual discipline. They resonate with the language of St Paul who contrasts the prayer in this life which produces 'puzzling images in a mirror' with the clarity of vision 'face to face', in a life after death. If the latter is the shape of our hope, prayer can be seen as the preparatory play, equipping its practitioners for the journey and helping to make sense of the experience as they imagine it may prove to be.

The notion of play as a way towards life after death receives some corroboration from most of the great world religions which have a creation myth that sees the original drama of creation as play undertaken by the first parent or God. The Aboriginal peoples of Australia tell of The Dream Time. The American Indians have a reverence for the world of nature of which they see themselves a part. The Muslims worship Allah who speaks into nothingness and allows the universe to result. The Hindu finds illusion, like a fine-spun spider's web, linking together human beings and material substance which will all vanish away and perhaps be re-spun. Meanwhile there is the image of Shiva as Lord of the Dance, Creator and Destroyer who bridges the movement between life and death.

The Judaeo-Christian story has many insights that begin with one version in the Book of Genesis, but throughout the Bible adds other metaphors or poems. All these are traps for the imagination, toys with which to build in meditative prayer, working out a pattern of light and dark. The most useful way of handling the divergent material is to treat them as poetic hints rather than conflicting dogmas that are set against each other. If the latter attitude rules then only one can be true and must emerge the victor. If instead of the either/or approach we can enjoy the diversity of the pictures, they might be better used as complementary insights, glimpses of the Maker at work, engaged in the play of creation, all designed to fill out the religious tapestry. This can then become an illustration of the inspired description of Wisdom as Creator which is imaginatively translated in the New Jerusalem Bible as

> I was beside the Master Craftsman,
> delighting in him day after day
> ever at play in his presence
> at play everywhere on his earth
> delighting to be with the children of men.
>
> (Proverbs 8. 30, 31)

It is a rich image of God at work, understanding him as displaying a divine counterpart to the freshness of human activity. It provides a useful contrast to the phrase from the Book of Daniel, 'The Ancient of Days' that has exercised a powerful influence on the Christian images of God, giving us the icons which eventually appear in the drawings of William Blake. It took the genius of Meister Eckhart, a German Dominican mystic of the fourteenth century, to provide a counterbalance with the thought; 'if God is eternal, God is eternally young'. Theology needs poetry to give expression to a levity and a playfulness that matches the weight and solemnity of the theological formulae in which the Church has needed to drape Divinity. The image of a God who plays can help the elderly let go of the guilt that they may mistakenly attach to their own unproductive activities.

Making the distinction between self-indulgent and useful play returns us to the parallel with the play of childhood through which a development to the next stage in life was achieved with the help of transitional objects. Might the 'play' of age be a way to handle the unknown, and therefore anxious, passage to a further stage of existence after death?

To follow this line of thought we need to recognize the intermediate or transitional objects upon which we relied while we engaged with life in its less problematic modes. For many, a discipline of prayer has been a way of staying open to the Transcendence, the awareness of the life of heaven. For myself the daily use of the Psalms has formed a habit of praise. For instance in some weeks of the year, the antiphon to the psalms each day draws on the words of Psalm 104.34: 'I will sing to the Lord as long as I live; I will praise my God while I have my being.' They can provide a kind of mantra that sings in one's head throughout the day, colouring the reaction to everything that happens. Overall the Psalms provide a record of the history of Israel seen in terms of salvation for which God is to be praised. The story of the release from Egypt is repeated in various forms in Psalm 114 or Psalm 66. Many of these hymns were written to be sung at great temple festivals that recalled the giving of the covenant on Mount Sinai to the People of Israel. Other psalms are more personal; for instance Psalm 77 is a prayer for help in sickness based upon the confidence that God, who has showed himself a saviour in the past, will still prove faithful to the relationship that he has established with both individual and nation.

The writer of the psalm moves between his personal distress and the history of God's dealings with his people:

> In the day of my trouble I sought the Lord;
>   my hands were stretched out by day and night and

> did not tire;
> I refused to be comforted. (v. 2)

This contrasts with:

> By your strength you have redeemed your people;
> The children of Jacob and Joseph. (v. 15)

and

> You led your people like a flock;
> By the hand of Moses and Aaron. (v. 20)

The confidence to cope with the present sickness is based on God's track-record in the past. If this has been the content of a person's prayer down the years, it becomes a foundation on which the relationship with God can continue and can carry him or her through the uncertain wilderness that makes up the twilit frontier. It is the same message that emerges from Psalm 126.

> When the Lord restored the fortunes of Zion
> Then were we like those who dream.
> Then was our mouth filled with laughter
> And our tongue with shouts of joy.
>
> Those who sowed with tears
> Will reap with songs of joy.
> Those who go out weeping, carrying the seed
> Will come again with joy, shouldering their sheaves.

The end of the play is to discover the harvest, the laughter and the delight which are the gifts of grace.

In one of his sermons John Donne offers such a dream of Heaven where all stress has been transcended. This embodies the kind of adult play that Winnicott might have recognized as desirable. It finds its parallel in the tranquillity of great art, as a painting or a poem finds its completion in a finished whole. In the making there may have been tension in the struggle to bring the colour and the design into a unity. The final piece may still illustrate the contradictions but always held in balance, for without this the work could not have been a place to rest and to respond. So too with a poem; sometimes one striking phrase claims the page, but not like a red gash on a field of grey. Other words must lead up to it and the design support it. So Donne describes the delight of the perfect life of Heaven which sounds as though it is the result of playing with an assortment of images, an understanding of contemplation as a way of holy play. Just as the image of God is dominated by the solemnity of 'the Ancient of Days', so too prayer can become a mirror of the medieval act of fealty, kneeling, hands together, eyes closed. It might better be understood as the open eyes, the dance of either body or spirit as music plays, vision or imagination focused on objects of delight: in this vein Donne writes:

> They shall awake as Jacob did and say as Jacob said, Surely the Lord is in this place and this no other but the house of God and the gate of Heaven. And into that gate they shall enter and in that house they shall dwell where there is no Cloud nor Sun, no darkness nor dazzling but one equal light, no noise or silence but one equal music, no fears nor hopes but one equal possession, no foes or friends but one equal communion and identity, no ends nor beginnings but one equal eternity. (XXIV Sermons, 1660)

A friend with whom I had been discussing the notion of the element of play involved in contemplative prayer rang to tell me an account of a retired priest living in a clergy home who was visited by friends. 'What do you do all day?' they asked. 'Wait for the resurrection' was the reply to which they said, 'Jack, can't you be more positive?' The work ethic seems alive and well in some clergy retirement houses! The American Indians hang in their windows 'dream-catchers' constructed of willow, feathers and coloured beads to entice the good dreams and exclude nightmares. Perhaps clergy homes deploy 'angel catchers' at their windows to prevent any subversive or playful thoughts infiltrating the sanitized air.

5

Lifelong Learning

Books, music, drama, pets and hobbies, all the apparatus of play can make an important contribution to the enrichment of old age. Through them we leave behind the values of the world of work which are calculated in terms of outcomes and results. Instead we move into a context where we enjoy an activity in its own right. In Chapter 4, Permission to Play, we argued for the serious quality of play and fantasy as an ingredient in retirement; at the same time, however, there is the conviction that those years should also include the stimulation of lifelong learning. This requires a careful look at what is meant by education. The traditional assumption has been that education belongs to the early years of life when learning takes place for a child in the family, followed by school. If this process is successful there is a further process of being equipped for work by university, training for a professional qualification or apprenticeship. After that, study is over and the person joins the workforce or is launched on his or her career.

In the present climate this attitude is changing. Not everyone had the opportunity to pursue the studies that they wished in childhood or adolescence. Gaps that arose then can be filled at any time in later life and further studies can be added to the curriculum. The Open University was the beginning of a new approach; this has been followed by the local colleges with open access courses and the various training schemes designed to get the young unemployed into work or helping older people back to a job. It is this latter aim of being equipped for employment that can take over the idea of lifelong learning and attach it irrevocably to the acquiring of new qualifications. These may be related to additional aspects of trades or else, in a career like teaching, the qualified person can bolt on additional skills that take him or her into new fields. Even after professional qualifications have been left behind we read accounts of sprightly 70-year-olds adding a new subject to their studies. We applaud a grandparent launched bravely into cyberspace. But that is not the sum total of what lifelong learning should be. There is another kind of learning that contributes to wisdom rather than information or knowledge. It comes by putting oneself at risk in trying out new skills or adopting a new role, failing and growing as the result of one's mistakes. In some ways this is more akin to the understanding of play.

The process of learning has two dimensions that can be related to the inner and outer world, and these need to be distinguished from each other. For instance, a history teacher may find it useful to add a new qualification in field archaeology which lets him take his class on a dig in the summer holidays. By contrast, a counsellor may find it helpful to work at understanding one special aspect of child abuse so that she can bring a particular insight to cases where something more is needed than her personal gifts of empathy. However, rather than acquiring additional pieces of intellectual information this may involve her in exploring aspects of her inner sexuality so that she has a deeper range of emotional responses. That requires inner learning, not undertaken in a classroom but involving a process of reflection and self-awareness which is an enrichment of the personality. It is a process that is recognized in other spheres; the poet takes an experience and gives it a new meaning by setting it alongside another image that fills out the first. A new light dawns because the unexpected pictures are set side by side. This is no longer a logical process; the poet's imagination works intuitively to take the reader by surprise, making an unexpected connection that illuminates the subject by its freshness. Something similar to this occurs in painting. The artist sees colour or shape in his or her own distinctive way and captures it for others to appreciate. This is particularly marked in the work of the surrealists. The art of Salvador Dalí takes this almost to the point of caricature. His paintings are sometimes described as 'illusions' because they carry a double portrayal. In one instance there is an overt portrayal of a battle scene; on a closer inspection something quite different emerges, the mouth and nose of President Lincoln. Here Dalí is drawing attention to the fact that all art differs from photography by adding a new perception that does not become apparent to the casual observer. Is he also making a political comment about Lincoln's involvement in the American Civil War, perhaps attributing the battles to the President's moral determination to abolish slavery?

To understand the trick of the 'illusion' is a matter for a practised eye. The quality of deeper vision which relates events at different levels to one another can be one of the gifts acquired in old age, but it may need to be cultivated with the help of another person. When we have lived our life focused on the obvious and explicit, the shift to the question of what is going on beneath the surface and listening to the music behind the words requires a fresh kind of attention. This is what makes a statesman rather than a politician, a prophet rather than a clever operator.

To acquire these new skills of insight will also be crucial to any kind of development in personal relationships. It is not sufficient, for instance, to observe that I have had a row with a colleague. As well as understanding the overt reasons for the difference, I need to ask what unconscious elements contributed to the conflict. Without this I am liable to recount the incident to others in the hope that they will agree that I am in the right. What might have become an occasion of personal growth becomes a recruiting campaign for supporters. Equally if I am introduced as a third party into a dispute on the assumption that I will support one side or the other, this would be to collude with the win/lose assumption on which both parties are operating. Reconciliation will spring from an honesty about what is happening at every level in the argument, so that both parties can appreciate what really lies between them and address the whole issue rather than the superficial differences. This is as true in international conflict as it is in personal disagreement, which is why the reporting of affairs by the tabloid press in black and white terms is so actively unhelpful. Is it possible to expect older people to bring their wisdom to bear and look behind the label of what is said? Do they have the maturity to offer mediation rather than join in the fight?

An effective contribution to the work of reconciliation requires first an understanding of the theory of human inter-action, and then personal experience of such situations, so that the new method of learning depends partly on an intellectual grasp of the process and partly on a casework approach, review-ing the mistakes and successes of one's contributions with the help of an outside observer.

As we all live longer and have more time to allow relation-ships to deepen there will be an increasing need for those who have skills in listening and discernment. Sometimes training for such expertise may be formally offered through specifically targeted organizations. In the case of marriage counselling there are bodies now called Relate (England) and Couple Counselling (Scotland) which have become the new incarnations of Marriage Guidance. At other times church or secular agencies offer to recruit and equip people to provide counselling in a general or specialist field. Courses in the art of mediation are now being offered by a number of agencies. These encourage volunteers to offer their time to work with neighbours who are at odds; there are projects to help reduce the incidence of bullying in schools. Those who have survived various crises in life are encouraged to act as mentors to others who are encountering the same dif-ficulties or are beginning along a similar path of development.

This is an ideal way for older people to contribute their accu-mulated wisdom to the community, always provided that they are willing to accept the appropriate induction and supervision. Such a procedure will ensure that they find the experience rewarding and at the same time enriching for others. It matches up with the requirement set out in the conclusions of the UN International Year of The Older Person that self-fulfilment should be one of the guiding principles. This is not, however, the same as self-congratulation; one of the prerequisites of learning is the willingness to be questioned about one's contributions. What lies behind them? Are we prepared to rethink them? Humility about oneself is the starting point for an ability to be of use to others.

Once again the Psalms offer a place where reflection about this kind of involvement can begin. As this section was in mind the Lectionary pointed me to Psalm 1 and I read:

1 Happy are they who have not walked in the counsel
     of the wicked,
   nor lingered in the way of sinners,
   nor sat in the seats of the scornful!

2 Their delight is in the law of the Lord,
   and they meditate on his law day and night.

3 They are like trees planted by streams of water,
   bearing fruit in due season, with leaves that do not
     wither;
   everything they do shall prosper.

4 It is not so with the wicked;
   they are like chaff which the wind blows away.

5 Therefore the wicked shall not stand upright when
     judgement comes,
   nor the sinner in the council of the righteous.

6 For the Lord knows the way of the righteous,
   but the way of the wicked is doomed.

Because the original thought comes from a psalm, it conjures up the picture of a little hermitage at the end of a village. In contemporary terms a small flat in a retirement complex might give a context to which it is easier to relate. The old person living there reflects on the patterns of life around. The sound of the children playing comes through the windows. She or he has learned to interpret the background noises as well as the words. The generations call bringing the news; the local gossip, the machinations of the neighbours in their different groups, the political point-scoring, the whispered hints of corruption. There are speculations about the love life of the young and their parents.

Perhaps these are as revealing about those who purvey the rumours as about the imagined actors. 'You have to make your own judgements,' reflects the hermit.

'What does it all add up to?' is the question. So much indignation by some, so much energy expended by others on ensuring the triumph of what they feel is so important, but it really matters hardly at all. Their cherished aims may even produce contrary results that they will regret in the long run. There are the struggles between those who desperately want a cause to win and others equally determined to stop it. Would not the whole community be happier without all the scheming, the campaigning and, in the last resort, sometimes, the lies and the deceit?

> Happy are they who have not walked in the counsel of
>   the wicked,
> nor lingered in the way of sinners,
> nor sat in the seats of the scornful!

I can see what that might mean when it comes to the cheating and deceit, but what about 'sitting in the seats of the scornful'? Does that mean that we are actually not meant to criticize other people? Should the observer ask: 'Is it as bad to sit here passing judgement on them as to have joined in their shenanigans? After all it doesn't help if there is a smug old person in the block claiming to have a corner in virtue. That could really put folk off. It could be a serious kind of hypocrisy.' The poetry of the psalm moves from the negative, undesirable qualities to the theme of delight. 'Their delight is in the law of the Lord.' They put their energy into the positive and inviting activity, they 'meditate on God's law day and night'. This is not about stopping their opponents from acting but looking instead towards a better alternative. The law of God is a programme for growth, not a negative barrage of criticism from the outraged. There is so much more to ensuring that a tree flourishes than stopping unwanted developments. My garden gets its attraction from all that has been planted there, not from the back-breaking efforts of weeding, necessary though that is.

The neighbourhood needs to leave behind all the bitterness

and to concentrate on all that comes from the delight of having good tenants, enjoying the contribution that they make to the community life.

> They are like trees planted by streams of water,
> bearing fruit in due season, with leaves that do not wither;
> everything they do shall prosper.

If the constructive neighbours are an encouragement to everyone else, is it too difficult to leave the rest to God? After all, the Psalm promises that he is aware of the misdeeds of the others:

> It is not so with the wicked;
> they are like chaff which the wind blows away.

A last honest admission might be: 'I feel that God is a bit slow in making his disapproval plain! People get away with an awful lot while we wait for God to make up his mind.'

That hermit's house or flat feels like a place where too many of us might be at home, majoring in the negative observations. No one is so charitable that they avoid all temptations to criticize; what matters is that the person who indulges in it should have the grace to ask questions about him or herself as well. The danger comes when we divide the human race into the good and the bad, the saved and the damned and worst of all assume that we are the ones upon whom God smiles.

It does no harm to visit the hermit in our imagination provided we listen to all that the old man says and do not stop with his criticism of a corrupt society. Mostly the same folk contribute to the light as to the dark. In the end we are the ones who are chiefly responsible for our characters, however much we find it convenient to put the blame on others.

The old observer of the psalm has the choice of how to respond to the gossip that is brought along. As the discernment is made whether to retain and savour the gossip, as though it was fruit that was good to eat, or to reject what is judged as actively poisonous, the various generations who call may take their cue from what they see is happening. An old person without any formal role can provide a moral litmus-test of what makes for enjoyment and what for disgust. He or she becomes an architect of society for good or ill.

Beyond the informal opportunities for contributing to a healthier community there are more structured ways in which opportunities are offered as aspects of 'volunteering'. The inducement they offer is the self-fulfilment that comes from redeploying skills built up in one sphere to be used in another. As I left being the Bishop of St Andrews I was invited to take over as the chairman of Age Concern Scotland. The constitution allowed me two terms of three years each and in that time I was introduced to the workings of a major charity and a significant employer. I encountered aspects of company law, finance and employment legislation that had never engaged my attention as a bishop, and I might have made a better bishop had I known them earlier. But even now I can listen to church problems with fresh insight.

Precisely because we are living longer and healthier lives there is, as never before, a pool of vitality out there in the community in its senior echelons. Society should not waste it and the elderly should not allow their expertise to be squandered. There is a barrier raised by age but society needs to encourage the retired to push this aside. There is a tradition of a false modesty which holds back the elderly from offering themselves as volunteers. It was once thought to be a virtue to be self-deprecating, but in the present circumstances of society, it is no longer appropriate to fear the reputation of being 'pushy'. There is a need for people to offer their services if they are able to support the more vulnerable in the community or champion a cause. At the same time this should not be seen as a grim duty but should be so structured that it provides both support and enjoyment. It is no shame for people to look for inducements to make their contribution. There is mutual benefit in the enrichment offered by volunteering. Society gets the immediate advantage of the service provided but also as that service contributes to the sense of well-being of the person who gives it, their attendance at the doctor's surgery and consumption of antidepressants will probably show a marked decrease.

Experience suggests that the beneficial effects arise from a combination of causes. The person involved feels wanted instead of devalued. The work is met with gratitude, loneliness and isolation are overcome, the volunteers have a sense of being part of a team with a shared purpose. This provides back-up and support to give confidence. When New Labour began to talk about 'the giving age' there was sound social sense in their strategy as a bridge-building exercise between individuals and age groups.

There is a sense in which this raises the fundamental question about the content of lifelong learning. What is the key lesson? If we have lived our lives within the competitive society, do we continue with the same motivation? Does the new agenda repeat the old incentive, to equip older people to come out top?

Would it be appropriate to have an award ceremony for The Grandparents of the Year, with the prize of a Saga cruise for the most adventurous surfers of the Internet? Or does that send the wrong signal? Is the object to inculcate the ideal of sharing and co-operation on the assumption that maturity sees the end of competition, and that therefore the integrators who work not for themselves but for others are those with most to offer by way of being role models to the younger generation? This is not simply a personal ideal. As older people become a higher proportion of the population, one corporate body, the University of the Third Age (U3A) has begun to organize national branches around Europe. Under its aegis people with skills offer to teach courses to their fellows without payment. Foreign languages, art, creative writing, musical appreciation, philosophy, theology, may all be on offer. Members may travel from one country to another and receive hospitality. Once again the stereotypes of age as stuck in the mud, unadventurous, limited are challenged and in the new liberation there is fun, health and vitality. It is not surprising that the U3A has grown significantly in every country in which it has been planted. It began on continental Europe with the intention of offering academic courses. In Britain the emphasis changed to include every kind of experiential learning, from woodworking to country walking. No academic standards were asked beforehand and no accreditation given at the end. The programme has about it some of the marks of play which were identified in Chapter 4.

Within the United States there is another organization with the title EASI, Environmental Alliance for Senior Involvement. Its counterpart in Scotland has the name Scottish Seniors Alliance for Volunteering for the Environment (SSAVE) and encourages pensioners to undertake tasks to monitor natural conditions or work at environmental projects. The motivation behind them is partly the concern for the damage to the ozone layer and its effects on human beings and climate change. Reflecting on this situation and the revolutionary new approach that it requires in contrast with the past, Monica Furlong, the religious journalist and broadcaster, wrote:

> Being human pushes us towards being daring, taking risks, to overreaching ourselves, to being the lone hero, to being stupendously strong, to being in control, powerful, to showing others, to fierce ecstasy either of anger or sexual conquest. Useless to pretend that we are not like that, that power and destruction are not exciting for us and part of our vitality.
>
> Being human inclines us to nurturing and protecting what is frail – a baby or a kitten – to feeding and nourishing, to offering comfort and support and wisdom, to the long patience of gestating the embryo in the womb, and the longer patience of nursing it in infancy. It inclines us to care for the earth itself and all its creatures. It likewise inclines us to trace the pattern of which we are a part. It makes us poets and painters, composers and playwrights, doctors and mothers.
>
> This is our double inheritance, but the first half of it, which may have been crucial to human survival now has to yield supremacy to the second inheritance, or there will be no babies, no kittens, no poets, no earth – just devastation. This the big change, the Great Task, the Eskimos say, upon which everything else depends. (Furlong, 1991)

As I have been involved with groups seeking to make that message heard, it has become clear that the generation most likely to take heed are the grandparents, the generation of the 'hollow trees' (see Chapter 2), urgent for the future of their grandchildren. They are not only the conservators but also the educators, teaching by example. Lifelong learning requires much more of older people today than adding on bits of intellectual information. It involves a new dynamic of concern which comes from an understanding of the opportunities and threats ahead. To revert to our earlier argument, we need an educated ability to play with the future.

Part of the curriculum is to discover fresh insights that set a person in context as part of the human family. The individual needs to appreciate his or her gifts and have the confidence to use them as a member of a valid, whole community. The process involves learning the internal trust that makes it possible to offer a contribution and also to trust the response of the human family group to the offer when it is made. Within the total dynamic of volunteering there is room for a great deal of mis-understanding which leaves disappointment and resentment in its wake. Old habits of self-effacement and placatory words die hard, but, because they do not convey the reality of the emotions involved, they do not achieve the proper level of communica-tion and so excuses have to be made: 'I did not like to put myself forward, but it would have been nice to be asked.' 'I did not want to impose on her, she is always so busy.' Meanwhile the unspoken questions arise: 'Did he think that I am not good enough, or past it?'

The final lesson to be learned is that of good communication. All through people's careers, within families, in working groups and public life, we fail to say what we really want to convey. In old age many of the regrets about the past stem from the lack of clarity that we allowed or accepted. Now is the chance at last to take the opportunity to 'speak what we feel, not what we ought to say'. There are occasions when people envy others their honesty. The lesson is there for all to take but because it carries a risk many choose to leave it till very late on, perhaps relegating it to the end of their curriculum for lifelong learning when it may prove to be too late.

6

Frailty and Faith

It is said that in the pulpit of the Wesley Chapel in London where John Wesley regularly preached, there was a written reminder: 'I preach as never sure to preach again, and as a dying man to dying men.' In his generation there was less need for a reminder of mortality, since disease continually took its toll from all age groups. Almost every family had a list of members who had died young. Their names were recorded on the tombstones in the graveyard of the local parish church. There was a similar feeling of impermanence among the young soldiers in the trenches in the First World War. When they came home on leave it was with a sense that there might not be another time. The feeling was captured by Julian Grenfell in his poem, 'Into Battle':

> The blackbird sings to him Brother, brother
> If this be the last song you shall sing
> Sing well for you may not sing another
> Brother sing.
>
> (Grenfell, 1939)

To-day, as life expectancy has increased, it is mostly with advancing years that people become aware of time running out. The number of visits to the doctor increase, accompanied by the lurking fear of some sinister diagnosis. These may be fuelled by disturbing accounts that appear in the press of the increasing incidence of such illnesses as prostate cancer. The reports carry the percentage figures of the population affected. Those with a mathematical and morbid turn may work out the odds on being one of those to whom they apply.

The pressure from such warning signals begins to build. Like shoppers faced with the threat of a shortage, who take to panic buying, fearful of what they might miss, older people may be concerned to cram as many experiences into the remaining time as possible in a way that seeks to deny death and hold it at bay. There is a culture of bravado which encourages the abandonment of stereotypes of ageing and urges a philosophy of 'growing old disgracefully'. How do we respond to this? Do we admire the spirit of those who refuse to be caged by social expectations or do we regret the loss of a graceful acceptance of reality? Once Benjamin Franklin could joke: 'In this world nothing can be said to be certain, except death and taxes.' Now few want to face explicitly the inevitability of death and it may be that this is because our society has lost the religious faith that once provided a framework to make the prospect bearable.

Recently evidence has begun to emerge that older people are no longer the bulwark of organized religion as once it had been assumed that they would be. Within the Christian churches they do not automatically support its observances as part of an accepted way of life or because they are perceived as addressing a felt need. The elderly are as open to doubt as any other age group. There are a number of possible explanations for this erosion of confidence in the traditional doctrines. Settled patterns of thought have been disturbed as science appears in popular estimation to have replaced the Bible as the explanation of the meaning and origin of life. Although there are sufficiently satisfactory intellectual explanations of the way through this dilemma, they have not carried popular conviction and the emotional certainty seems weakened. Perhaps also the years added to peoples' lives have left space to become disillusioned with the performance of the religious institutions, whether locally or internationally, and this has eroded the credibility of their doctrines. The communications revolution has opened an awareness of other world faiths, or alternative points of view. Initially people may have sought corroboration of their own beliefs in the teaching of other religions. When this has not been provided they may be left questioning the confidence that any belief system can inspire.

For some of these reasons people feel that they are enmeshed in a culture of uncertainty. Part of the knock-on effect is a similar loss of moral absolutes. Some groups, mostly religious in origin, are fighting a rearguard action to defend specific standards of conduct in sexual matters. They base their differences in moral convictions on variations in doctrinal systems. This arouses profound antagonisms between the alternative creeds. For instance the issue of homosexuality has produced this effect not only in interfaith dialogue but even between a variety of Christian theologies. As antagonism begins to mount, faith has to be found through a more rigorous intellectual search, capable of overcoming the emotions aroused when security is threatened. The discipline requires a more demanding effort than the traditional passive acceptance of unreflective faith. On the one hand that can be a most stimulating undertaking and something that enriches retirement. On the other, since it also involves letting go of easy certainties that have in the past provided comfort against chilly draughts, it can be a deeply resented discipline. Those who raise questions are stereotyped by the majority as destructive. Only a minority respond with gratitude for the stimulation they provide.

There is no longer a reassuring text which a pastor can with authority hand out as a mantra, to be repeated. People should be helped to find a personal insight that will engage their intellect and imagination and offer a persuasive argument that they can trust. Where then do they put their faith? It will begin in what they can understand and appreciate out of personal experience. Their creed must reflect what they have found for themselves to be true. Their understanding of God will incorporate their conceptions of justice, of love and forgiveness. The Old Testament recognized the logic of this with the question 'Shall not the Judge of all the earth do right?' But if the figure of the Judge as part of the Godhead has disappeared, where do they turn? Somewhere they need a scaffolding of belief that makes sense of all the pain and apparent injustice of human experience. Everyone has in their lives mourned the death of young people, the violation of innocence, and they have to acknowledge that they themselves have not always acted with integrity. Yet they want a world in which evil is overcome and the victory of the good ensured. Sometimes they have promised themselves a final judgement where everything will be put right. Sometimes they have looked for justice to be worked out in the course of history or even in one person's life. In an age when the majority no longer read the Bible for illustrations of justice at work, modern myths like Tolkien's *Lord of the Rings* or even the Harry Potter novels have provided a contemporary substitute for the demonstration of the victory of Truth and Goodness over Falsehood and Evil.

At the same time that people seem to be seeking such emotional reassurance, the voice of a poet like T. S. Eliot is reinforcing the fact that we do not know. He writes:

> Let me disclose the gifts reserved for age . . .
> And last, the rending pain of re-enactment
> of all that you have done, and been; the shame
> of motives late revealed, and the awareness
> Of things ill done and done to others' harm
> Which once you took for exercise of virtue.
> Then fools' approval stings, and honour stains.
>
> (Eliot, 1963)

If one listens to the performance of a Requiem, the music may be profoundly moving but the words, particularly relating to the theme of the Last Judgement no longer carry conviction. The prayer that the departed may be saved from the pains of Hell, the pit, the lion's mouth, the infernal regions seems overstated, almost hysterical. The words of the Middle Ages are no longer ours.

Similarly there is a gap between ourselves and our Victorian ancestors. In a century and a half religious assumptions have so changed that what once were edifying stories no longer carry conviction. I remember in childhood reading a tract which contained the story of Sir Walter Scott on his death-bed. He requested the Bible to be read to him. When asked what passage he replied, 'John 14, of course'. The anecdote was intended to convey the message that the famous novelist put his faith in the reported words of Jesus: 'I go to prepare a place for you . . . In my father's house are many mansions.' This was presumably recorded to encourage others in their faith.

In the contemporary world we ask why the convictions of a man in 1832 should have a bearing on our beliefs as we currently ask questions about the meaning of death. In the years between the tides of faith have ebbed and flowed. We no longer have a confidence that the Gospels contain the exact words that Jesus said. Maybe the Bible no longer carries the assurance that it did for Walter Scott, so that he cannot offer a role model. Yet, as the number of older people increases the churches and other bodies of believers want to offer the pastoral reassurance that will help people to live at peace with the inevitability of their death.

Where people feel that there are no longer confident examples of unconquerable reassurance they may seek to avoid the uncertainty by use of a mechanism of denial. There are residential homes for old people where the management seek to employ ways of distancing the other inhabitants from the death of a fellow member. Screens are placed round the bed, the undertakers come discreetly when people have been persuaded away from the scene, but the silence about the disappearance and the newly created absence cannot be avoided. The anxieties that each individual feels about their approaching end cannot be quieted by the institutional denial. Two options seem possible, either a Stoic acceptance of the unpalatable, or else to find a way in which those who hold a faith that explicitly looks forward to life after death can allow that faith to speak to their anxieties from within the practice of their religion. Can they find rituals or stories that absorb the fears and bring peace?

The American theologian, Paul Tillich, in his book, *The Courage to Be*, identified what he described as the three 'ontological anxieties' which hang over human existence. They are the fears of condemnation, annihilation and meaninglessness. By calling them 'ontological' he implied that they threaten the very core of a person's being and therefore have a special relevance in a discussion of Death which by its nature calls into question his or her continued existence. Whichever of these fears is the dominant factor in the psychological make-up of an individual will determine his or her primary response.

It is significant that the traditional funeral rites, especially

Christian ones, address all the three anxieties at different points in the service. First there is a commemoration of the life of the departed, his or her achievements are recorded, the mourners are invited to give thanks for all that he or she meant. A strong thread of meaning is asserted and there is an opportunity for all present to contribute to a shared acknowledgement of it. This is further expressed in the meticulous attention paid to the dead body, in acknowledgement of the inherent worth and significance of every human being each in a unique way.

In each life there are also elements for regret, and within the funeral service provision is made both for an exchange of forgiveness between the living and the departed and at the same time the dead are commended to the care and forgiveness of God who is recognized as 'Allah the all merciful' or 'the God and Father of our Lord Jesus Christ'. After the funeral is over, in some form or another, family members and friends gather and restore broken lines of communication or make up quarrels. This gives an emotional reality to the words about forgiveness spoken in the service.

Finally, the issue of survival that replaces the fear of annihilation is addressed either by the faith in a life after death or in the expectation of a reincarnation. In Christian terms the soul of the departed is commended into the hands of God with the implication that life continues. The names of the dead are also recorded with meticulous care because they are immortal souls to be remembered.

It seems clear that there will be no panacea which speaks to all. In Chapter 7 we will explore some of the ways in which a person can make provision for his or her funeral. The details of the particular occasion will reflect what death has come to mean to an individual over the years. Yet like so many serious concerns the answers may not emerge through addressing the broad philosophical or doctrinal issue, but may be read by implication from the practical details of the arrangements that are made or things that are done. What we do by custom at a funeral may help us discern what are the expectations, the beliefs or the nagging questions that have made them appropriate.

In an age dedicated to experimental proof it is not always sufficient to be able to argue an intellectual case for a doctrine such as life after death. This may explain the considerable interest taken in the reported 'near death experiences' that have appeared over the last 25 years beginning in the United States. The first of these studies, *Life after Life*, was written by a Dr Raymond Moody and described very similar sensations experienced by people who had been declared to be clinically dead but were subsequently revived. During that time they had been able to observe what was happening, usually in a hospital context, as resuscitation procedures were invoked. They were later able to give accurate reports of the detail of these. Meanwhile they had also experienced a journey along a dark tunnel towards a bright light which gave them a sense of reassurance: sometimes they met old acquaintances, sometimes the light was an angelic or perhaps divine figure. At some point they reported that they were turned back to resume life on earth. This was claimed by some as a proof of life after death: others, taking a stand more firmly in the empirical world, offered a theory that the process of dying might trigger a particular sequence in the brain that was translated into the phenomena reported by those who had not actually died.

The first point to be made in relation to the reports is that none of the people making them died. They are not post-mortem observations but belong to the human experience of the end of life, from whatever source they are derived. However desperate people are for reassurance, it will not do to cook the books to provide it.

The last word lies here with philosophy. Immanuel Kant argues that no conclusive knowledge can be gained about a reality which is not in space and time and is thus not the object of our perception. On this basis proofs for a life after death are theoretically impossible. 'All these conclusions of ours which profess to lead us beyond the field of possible experience are deceptive and without foundation' (*Critique of Pure Reason* (1781), quoted Küng, 1995). Professor Hans Küng of Tübingen himself goes on to amplify this

Indeed our reason spreads its wings in vain trying by the power of thought to get beyond the world of phenomena and come upon an eternal life. And not only do the trees not grow up to heaven, even the skyscrapers we plan and build so boldly fail to do so. At best they scrape the sky but they cannot open the heavens. (Küng, 1995: 9)

What then have the religious agencies to say to old people who want to have some map of the journey? Honesty denies recourse to any explicit statements. The pictures of Heaven and Hell that were the stock-in-trade of the medieval Church can no longer be defended. Yet there are urgent questions to be met. At least in Britain the ball is mainly in the court of the Christian churches who minister to the majority of the population. Their task is first of all to hear the anxieties and to understand them. After that there is the work with those who need to express their feelings in terms of liturgy, thinking about their funeral, designing their farewells and even as they go on adding years to their score, asking 'Who will be left to come?'

The most unhelpful attitude is to avoid the topic completely. Sometimes embarrassment for oneself or fear of creating a difficulty for other friends or family members stops the conversation. What is wanted however is an honest exploration of all the emotions, positive or negative.

A number of voices have expressed the importance of coming to terms with dying while we are still in good health. Professor Hans Küng writes of 'a spirituality of memento mori, which is not to stand as a gloomy threat over all life or at the end of life, but which makes another, perhaps even serene, basic attitude possible in the midst of life – for life'. Professor George Guiarchi of Southampton University makes a similar point with a dramatic account which, on occasions, he enacts, of an Italian friend who escorted him to the cellar of his house. There he took from the wall an empty coffin shell, he threw his arms around it and drummed with his fingers, ecstatically chanting: 'Embrace the coffin, embrace the coffin'. For him this was a symbol of liberation from a fear of death which he had now discarded. Why do some of the religions which have no reason to fear death allow it to assume such an importance? (Guiarchi, personal communication).

An old friend who is a retired army chaplain spoke about his disappointment with the home to which he has retired. 'I chose a place for retired clergy', he said 'because I hoped for some good theological conversation, but no one will talk about death. Dammit, I have always been curious about my next posting, but here nobody wants to think about what happens next!' It would be no help to him to be fed optimistic notions of near death experiences. He wants an honest appraisal of all that has filled theological discourse over the years, not Sunday-school stories but the questions that have been teased out by the intellect of believers whose faith has given them the courage to doubt slick answers.

Beyond the open theological issues, space also must be made for the intuitions that come with old age. It is a time when the curtain that separates the earthy from the spiritual world seems to grow thin. Old people think no less rigorously but nevertheless they have perceptions that can carry them into realms where angels become more real, communication with close friends and family seems to happen by the transference of thought, healing prayer assumes a more immediate potency. It may be that the barriers built up by mechanistic assumptions in the prevailing culture are removed or it may be that emotions are less inhibited and therefore have freer access to consciousness.

All these questions and affirmations need to be addressed by the churches and the religious bodies of the other faiths. Some may find that such issues are best handled in the private discourse of a faith community. They do not wish to engage with the language of secular society, but if they cannot find forms of expression that make sense in everyday living their audience will shrink to a small coterie who are already committed to their private language. The rest need to find their place as children of the shared secular culture and be enabled to reinterpret the beliefs of earlier generations in a new way. They need to be confident in accepting the data that accrues from old age and discovering its meaning in the common language of the culture. This will enable the whole family of a society to celebrate the insights that flow between children, parents and all those who contribute out of their greater age. This will bind together those who might fear, because of their increasing years, they were losing touch with the common discourse across the generations. At the same time, it might give a new richness of understanding to the young. A sense of division between young and old will take away the gifts they could have shared, while mutual appreciation will maximize the assets which can accrue to the developing discovery of age. This requires a conscious decision by society and its agencies to build on the gifts of age that are now becoming available. Just as a family is enriched by the inclusion of all generations into its life, so the community needs to take note of the anxieties that its older members feel as well as the gifts that they bring, and seek to ensure that they are included in the agenda which is concerned for the welfare of all the citizens whatever their age group.

As far as the churches are concerned a disproportionate amount of energy has been expended on catering for the young while the old have been taken for granted. Sunday schools have filled the church halls with their drawings while nobody has taken the time to help my old friend to imagine a mental map of his 'next posting'. I am not advocating the rival claims of one age group against another. The ideal is that the whole family should be assured a place in education and pastoral care. I have however detected an 'institutional ageism' in church bodies over the years. When I have discussed the make-up of a congregation seeking a new incumbent, they have met me with an apologetic attitude: 'We are afraid we are rather old. We need a young vicar with children of primary school age to bring in the young people.' That is not even psychologically true: I have known parishes which have flourished because they have responded to the ministry of spiritual grandparents, not members of their own age group.

Come on; let's celebrate the Old! In practical terms that means delighting in their company, hearing their stories, attending to their needs, using their language and being grateful for what they have to give. It is just possible that old people have begun to defect from the Church not because they disbelieve in God, but because they feel that the churches have begun to disbelieve in them.

If the churches are looking for a mission project for the new millennium here is one ready to hand, manufactured by the times in which we live. Such a project will require something more than campaign slogans. All who are concerned with old people need to form an alliance to take seriously the claims of spiritual growth. A wide range of people are professionally in touch with the old: nurses in hospitals, social workers in the community, home helps, clergy, doctors, visitors from various organizations. All need basic training to sensitize them to the hunger for a serious conversation that can be disguised under the cloak of a shopping request, a comment about the news or a bit of gossip about another person's illness. The response does not have to be in religious terms but simply appropriate to the idiom in which the question is phrased. Spirit speaks to spirit in a variety of ways. What matters is that such conversations should be understood and not allowed to go unheeded.

Many more than currently achieve it may be ready for some mountaineering of the soul. Because it is a lost art for those in the heartlands of life, there is a need for a corps of Sherpas of the Spirit who are ready to accompany those who are want to travel. The journey is depicted in different religions by various images. I know too little of other faiths to work freely with their literature, but their language is of pilgrimage, explorations and silence.

Those who wonder about the future are apt to keep the questions to themselves, perhaps because they are unsure how the questions will be received. Religious clichés would be a disheartening response, so would an embarrassed silence. It may seem that the adventure is best explored in the hints and metaphors of poetry rather than the definitive statements of theology. I tried to express some of this in a 'Rite of Passage'.

> From the taffrail of his cot-bed side,
> he scanned the bone-locked sea of memory,

whose grey surface smoothed away
drowned faces,
places lost beyond recall.

Captain of his last trip, he hauled the sheets
to catch the light airs of his failing lungs
and make his landfall on the further shore . . .

Body-focused attendants missed
the intensity of purpose.
Nurses taking for sweat
the sea-spray of his inner journey,
tucked a thermometer
to replace his telescope;
a priest paddled past, encrusted with clichéd foam

The captain's urgent signal
found the watch unmanned;
only civilians, unskilful to decode
received his flickering light.

Then the setting sun drew a straight course of gold
across the waves;
the energy of angels
held his bows steady
and from the taut rigging plucked
a requiem for his safe homecoming.

(Hare Duke, 1994)

W. H. Auden's 'Christmas Oratorio' with its invitation to the surprising journey is another encouragement to adventure in unlikely places. He would not have claimed a firm membership of the Christian Church but speaks for the risk-taking constituency of the human spirit. We need to draw into the circle of discourse all whom we can and all who appreciate the exercise, which is the true spirituality of old age.

7

Preparing a Funeral

The idea of making arrangements for one's own funeral may seem surprising to some people. 'But I won't be there!' is a likely reaction. On the other hand the process of dying, at least when it is approached though ageing and illness, is a journey to be made and managed with grace and perhaps humour. There is evidence that within a family or close group it has an important part to play in helping forward the grief work that attends a death.

This has not always been the perception. In the days when the Church and its doctrines held sway in society, it was assumed that funerals would be conducted according to the rites prescribed in the official service books and that the minister who conducted them would necessarily be an ordained clergyman. The only exception were the Quakers, the Society of Friends, founded by George Fox in the middle of the seventeenth century.

The process of preparation began, not at death, but in a time of sickness when, for instance, it was written into the Church of England Prayer Book that the priest visiting a sick person should question him or her about all temporal affairs and personal relationships:

> Then shall the minister examine whether he repent him truly of his sins and be in charity with all the world; exhorting him to forgive from the bottom of his heart all persons that have offended him; and if he hath offended any other, to ask them forgiveness; and where he hath done injury or wrong to any man, that he make amends to the uttermost of his power.

After that, the instructions continue, 'and if he hath not before disposed of his goods, let him then be admonished to make his

Will and to declare his debts . . . for the better discharging of his conscience and the quietness of his Executors.'

All these provisions assume the presence of a suitable guide to accompany the sick person in his self-examination. Because it is also presumed that this person will be a priest, a form of confession and absolution is provided. In addition there is a chance for the patient to affirm the Creed and then to hear read Psalm 71 which is full of comfort and reassurance. It begins

> In thee O Lord have it put my trust; let me never be put
> to confusion,

and ends

> Forsake me not, O God, in mine old age, when I am gray-headed; until I have shewed Thy strength unto this generation and Thy power to all them that are yet for to come.
> Thy righteousness O God is very high, and great things are they that Thou hast done; O God who is like unto Thee.

This 'Order for the Visitation of the Sick' had its origins in a much older tradition than the Reformation or even the medieval Church. In the Celtic Church the task of seeing a person through the time of his or her death belonged not necessarily to a cleric but the *anam-chara* or soul friend who would be summoned for the rite which was variously called 'the soul-leading', 'the soul-peace' or 'the soul-soothing'. This close friend had a special place afterwards in the family of the person who had died.

Within the Buddhist tradition there is a similar ritual to be carried out at a death-bed. In what is known as *The Tibetan Book of the Dead*, 'there is a unique form of knowledge used to provide the guidebook or travelogue of the after-death states which is designed to be read by a master or spiritual friend to a person as the person dies and after death' (Rinpoche, 1998). The *bardo*, or transitional state, to which this specifically applies is the difficult transition at the time of dying. Alongside this there are three other less dramatic *bardo* periods identified as:

1. The natural process of human life between birth and death.
2. The luminous process of the after-death experience.
3. The process of preparing for the next rebirth.

Because these are more diffused, they do not require the specific presence of a skilful guide to work with the individual at a moment of crisis. It is noticeable that in relation to death there is a similarity of purpose in the aims of the traditional practices, Buddhist and Celtic Christian. They are:

1. to focus the mind of the dying person on the assurance of the teaching in which they have been formed;
2. to accompany the individuals personally as they start on the unknown path;
3. to centre their attention on the promised future.

Quite apart from the theological expectations of life after death, there is a great advantage in being able to speak about what is happening in the present. Too often the closeness of death is unacknowledged. The game of silence is mostly justified by those who keep the secret, as a way of protecting others from a truth that is too painful. If, however, it can be explored both the dying person and those about to be bereaved may find it a mutually healing exchange.

In our present society the death at home that is envisaged by the old traditions, Celtic Christian, Buddhist, Anglican and others, is becoming a rarity, perhaps almost a luxury. Instead of the re-assurance of a familiar place and known faces, most people will have been hurried into a hospital ward on the assumption that the best care is available there and that any possible medical intervention that is required will be immediately on hand. The prime interest is to prevent death occurring, not to provide the ideal conditions in which it can be faced. The oxygen mask takes precedence over the last rites. The message conveyed in the hospital dramas on television is that death is a battleground. When it threatens, it is confronted with frenzied activity. The collapse of a patient is the cue for alarms to sound, and the 'crash team' to rush into action with sophisticated equipment. We watch defibrillators deployed, injection of stimulants and as a last resort chest-thumping massage. As was suggested in Chapter 1, this priority is likely to reflect the needs of the family or the fears of the medics rather than the wishes of the patient. From his point of view it might be more helpful to return to the step-by-step ritual of the Prayer Book or the Tibetan *bardo* practice which recognizes that the moment of death should not be disturbed because something very important is going on beyond human sight.

While twenty-first-century attitudes have pushed aside the tradition of preparing spiritually for death, economic anxiety has opened another door to a discussion of the subject. There is a mounting concern about the cost of a funeral. The result are schemes which encourage people to invest in a prepaid funeral plan. This, claim the advertisers, not only takes care of the considerable expense of the event but also saves the mourning relatives the stress of making arrangements for the service while they are coping with their loss. This latter claim needs to be examined; it can prove a doubtful benefit taking away as much as it gives. On the one hand, to plan one's funeral in advance may contribute to an individual's sense of control and allow him to set the mood he desires by the ritual, the music and the hymns. It will also allow for any particular beliefs to find expression rather than be subsumed in the blanket formula of the expected and undisturbing that the undertaker is likely to advise. The disadvantage is that this also takes away from the family what can be an integral part of their mourning process, even if the general pattern of the service has been discussed with the patient beforehand. Because death is mostly a taboo subject, it catches people unprepared and they hand over decisions to the professionals, clergy and undertakers, without appreciating the significance of the funeral details which convert a general rite of passage into a personal farewell. If they can hold on to the process, it can be a helpful experience. But it may be that coming suddenly to such a point can be an emotionally overwhelming task. It then feels that the professionals have an important role. If nobody in the family has considered the subject beforehand, a funeral mostly sends people back to folk memories or old orders of service if any have been collected in the family archives. The choice of hymns runs out after *Crimond* and 'Abide with me'; any innovation is feared because somebody might be offended. The paralysis of the unfamiliar takes hold and inhibits fresh thinking. This is when clergy and undertakers can break this log-jam by setting out the present realities and what is on offer.

Once it is appreciated how much is now a matter of personal choice rather than prescribed ritual a whole host of options open up. Quite apart from the form and content of the service, the burial site does not have to be a cemetery nor is a crematorium the only other option to a graveyard burial. Scotland has always accepted that a person might be buried on their own land. Now woodland sites are available. Coffins can be woven from willow and need not be the expected product of a funeral director's catalogue. Alternatively they can be constructed of strong cardboard which will be more easily biodegradable. A friend can be invited to decorate such a coffin with hand-painted flowers. If advice about alternatives is not easily available locally it can be obtained through the Natural Death Centre (20 Heber Road, London NW2 6AA, phone 020 8208 2853, rhino@dial. pipex.com).

Current practice endeavours to ensure that the rights of various consumer groups, rail travellers, hospital patients and shoppers among them, are protected and relevant charters have been compiled. Through the National Funerals College a *Dead Citizens Charter* has been drawn up to ensure that at death the services offered shall be neither exploitative, undignified nor inadequate.

Whilst the emphasis is now being put on choice and perhaps the idea of a customized funeral, it needs to be remembered that the occasion is not a private ceremony, simply tailored to the whim of the one person who has died. All the family and friends need the occasion as part of their farewell. According to the impact of a person's life a wider community may need to participate in the sense of loss and of gratitude.

A friend who died recently had meticulously crafted his own funeral. It gave him great satisfaction to know that nothing was left to chance. For the most part this was an act of great kindness. Nevertheless, in his careful preparation he left many of his friends unable to express the tenderness that they had felt for him and their sorrow at his going. Other funerals have been used by the person who has died to make a theological point. Sometimes the arrangements have embodied an explicit criticism of a revised liturgy or repudiated the ordination of women by excluding female colleagues from sharing in the funeral rites. This has left the sourness of controversy to embitter the occasion rather than bring a sense of reconciliation. Such issues matter so little where the hope is of new life. A funeral should be an invitation to a journey on which there will be no winners or losers and therefore a chance to let go of the hooks that grapple a person to the shores of old controversies.

If the funeral is to be planned in advance and all the options considered, it might be possible for a person before death to gather an intimate group of family or friends help him or her to devise an imaginative farewell. The reactions of others would give a useful sounding-board to judge the proposals. The ritual contents of the service are not as restrictive as most people suppose. Readings can be chosen from stories, from favourite poetry, from the lyrics of songs. Music can be popular or classical, sacred or secular. In the service there can be a time of silence, or a space for music while the mourners recall their personal memories. All the relatives might be given the opportunity to express their preferences, to share in the choice of the ingredients which add meaning to the framework of any rite. Thought should be given to silence as well as words, the visual symbols and perhaps the venue that best expresses what needs to be said at that funeral.

The criteria for a good farewell seem to include a compassionate sympathy with all who have found the person difficult, a willingness to laugh at one's failures and to see how things might have been managed better and above all the exchange of forgiveness. Giving liturgical expression to such emotions requires patient discussion and much forbearance, but as life begins to show signs of reaching its end this could be the most important undertaking. An honest, perhaps humorous discourse can evolve which gives an opportunity for reminiscence and will begin the mourning process in a helpful way. In old age, as self-esteem diminishes with the perceived reduction of either power or significance, it is right to remember the achievements of the past, the family successes, the good holidays, even the delight in household pets and their various personalities. What might once have seemed boastful can now be the subject of delight and thanksgiving. In old age one does not want to crow, 'Haven't I done well!', but simply to comment, 'I have been so lucky' or 'so blessed!' It can be a chance to thank one's friends as well as involve them in a discussion of profound import and to build an opportunity for good human communication which could lead into the mutual forgiveness as the Prayer Book suggests. By this means, understanding will be increased because the reasons for choices once baffling can be explored, not left to be confronted without explanation after the person has died. Non-communication in the silence that follows a death is the soil in which resentment grows.

Such a time of preparation might occupy a single occasion or perhaps it would be better extended over a period of weeks. It would be the contemporary equivalent of the intervention of the soul friend. The dying person will have the chance to review his life, its delights and regrets.

It has been said of the Gaelic tradition that at every turn there is a vein of hospitality including the welcome in the next world. 'Once across the dark river of dying, the soul escapes the pains and weariness of the body and is met by friendly emissaries of heaven. A guardian angel leads the soul upwards . . . and the Archangel Michael is there to offer a hospitable welcome in the friendly heavenly household.' One of the songs for dying had the words:

> Be every saint and sainted woman in heaven,
> O God of the creatures and god of the goodness,
> Be taking charge of you in every strait,
> Every tide and turn you go.

Be each saint in heaven,
Each sainted woman in heaven
Each angel in heaven
Stretching out their arms for you,
Smoothing the way for you
When you go yonder
Over the river hard to face;
When you go yonder home
Across the river hard to face.

Be the Father reaching out for you
In his fragrant clasp of love,
When you go over the river in spate
Of the black river of dying.

(Jones, 1994: 193)

In the same vein, the New Funeral Rites of the Scottish Episcopal Church include the commendation, based on earlier tradition but re-crafted:

Go forth upon your journey from this world,
dear child of God,
into the hands of the Father who made you,
to find life in Christ who redeemed you,
to rejoice in the Spirit who renews you.
May the heavenly host sustain you,
and the company of the redeemed enfold you.
May peace be yours this day,
and the heavenly city your home.

If such a sense of welcome can be accepted as part of dying then it makes sense to let the farewell have about it an atmosphere of celebration. One such occasion is documented in a remarkable book published in 1997 which gives an account of a dying university professor by one of his former students, Mitch Albom. Albom had already a strong affection for Morrie Schwartz who had taught him at university 20 years before. By chance he learns that Morrie was dying of a degenerative neurological disease, ALS or amyotrophic lateral sclerosis. Mitch was a professional journalist. After making the discovery of Morrie's illness he attended every week at the Schwartz house to work with his old tutor as the only student on what he describes as a course on the Meaning of Life. The account he has produced reflects his professional skill. He sums up the spirit of the former university teacher whom he has now come to address as 'coach'; 'as he was dying he was intent on proving that the word "dying" was not synonymous with "useless".' It was this which lay behind one significant occasion that Albom recounts:

> The New Year came and went. Although he never said it to anyone, Morrie knew this would be the last of his life. He was using a wheelchair now, and he was fighting time to say all the things he wanted to say to all the people he loved. When a colleague at Brandeis [his university] died suddenly of a heart attack, Morrie went to his funeral. He came home depressed.
>
> 'What a waste' he said. 'All those people saying all those wonderful things and Irv never got to hear any of it.'
>
> Morrie had a better idea. He made some calls. He chose a date, and on a cold Sunday afternoon, he was joined in his home by a small group of friends and family for a 'living funeral'. Each of them spoke and paid tribute to my old professor. Some cried. Some laughed.
>
> Morrie cried and laughed with them. And all the heartfelt things we never get to say to those we love, Morrie said that day. His 'living funeral' was a rousing success. (Albom, 1997: 12)

This is a pattern which might be followed with great profit. In earlier times a family would gather to take leave of a father who was dying. In my own experience I had a friend who was dying of cancer. Within a few months of his death, he hosted a gathering on his birthday which all knew would be his last party: it was a warm and convivial occasion full of good memories from the past, anecdotes to savour and farewells which acknowledged that he was going on a long journey. He also asked me to write something that might help his grandchildren to come to terms with his death. For myself it was an enormous joy to put into words something of my love, admiration and sadness, so that he could read and share them while he was still alive and perhaps from them draw some comfort for the journey as well as use them for his family. (The text of what was written appears in the Appendix at the end of the chapter.)

The suggestion that has been explored above of a gathering to plan a funeral service might be another occasion for this kind of exchange. Since friends and family could bring their suggestions for readings and reminiscence, it might be a more focused opportunity to acknowledge hurts and exchange forgiveness. If we are ready to speak of death, to look it in the eye, then we will do well to establish some models which can be agreed, so that if they are adopted as customs, they may help us speak what we feel without embarrassment because they have become a tried and accepted path for support. It is a question of establishing good practice and building on it.

The first decision to be made is 'What is the point of a funeral service?' This can be a genuine theological dilemma. Some people may see it as a rite of passage which is required to be carried out in accordance with precedent. It is fundamentally addressed to the supernatural world, a kind of magical formula ensuring a welcome for the deceased. Certainly some of the medieval ceremonies like the Absolution of the Dead bear all the marks of this. Yet the basic Christian theology is that every person is to be recognized as the child of God who needs no extra ceremonies to claim the love that belongs to him by grace and not because of anything that he has done to earn it.

The more contemporary attitude sees the words and symbolism of the funeral directed to the mourners. What is done is designed to help them to cope with their emotions and begin the tasks of mourning. On this premise the event can be tailored to meet the needs and employ the skills of the mourners. For instance at a recent funeral an 11-year-old grandchild read a poem that she had written to celebrate her grandfather. On another occasion, after a cot death, the distraught parents could not find any traditional reading for use at the service; the priest suggested that they write a letter to their child expressing their unfulfilled hopes for him. What might have been either a repressed and depressing or an emotionally over-charged occasion became a cathartic and helpful event. Funerals need to be liberated from the strait-jacket of conformist religiosity which empties them of the power that could be theirs.

I once presided at the funeral of a controversial politician who had been a sign of division in the country where he had worked for the Head of State. The President had been deposed and in his fall this man had been brought down and for a short while imprisoned. He had also put his legal expertise at the service of other states who in his life had been slow to recognize him. Yet at this funeral in an Anglican church in London, the coffin was carried in to the sound of African talking drums which celebrated his achievements in the country which had imprisoned him; a delegation arrived breathless off a plane from a country whose constitution he had drafted, the opposing political parties of the United Kingdom were represented and, by his direction, while his coffin went to the crematorium, drinks were served in the adjoining church hall. This man was not an explicit churchgoer but his funeral in which he had made space for apology and celebration had about it a liberating quality which was for me an essential demonstration of the gospel.

Do we all need the conscious awareness that there will be friends to celebrate the end of one's life, to remember the kindnesses that one did, the courage that one showed, the generosity and the humour or whatever one's good points may have been? This could help us to move on and recall the faults, the mistakes, the unkindness and to meet them with forgiveness, bring together the honest acknowledgement of failure and the gratitude for the warmth of human affection that have made up one's life. I have often thought that the ideal funeral sermon, if one is to be preached, should say in essence: 'He was a bit of a stinker, but we loved him' or put in a more acceptable theological dress:

> Beside the tale of good things done
> We know the faults, the hurt, the blame,

And pray, dear God, for everyone
The healing given in Jesus' name.

Since at the end both dark and light
Dapple the death we bring to you,
May Christ whose cross sets wrong to right,
In risen power make us anew.

Appendix

The Scots Pine

The old tree had stood as a focal point on the skyline for as long as the woodland creatures could remember. For some it had provided shelter in its roots or branches, others had fed off its cones and shoots. It had been a direction point for high flying birds as they homed on the Black Wood. Now a sudden violent gale had overturned it and the animals had gathered to mourn the loss and remember all that it had meant to them.

A pair of capercaillie recalled its spring shoots rich with the turpentine tasting sap; squirrels remembered summer games along its branches; red deer told of family legends about the tree when it had been a sapling and how it had given shelter and food in long winters. As the stories followed one on the other they became a long catalogue of loss. The gathering was so overwhelmed by sadness that the gifts and the guidance provided by the pine in the past were being washed away in present grief.

The long-eared owl whose parents had nested in the pine and who had taken his first lessons in flying from its branches, was made of sterner stuff.

This is no way to celebrate a noble member of the woodland. There is too much concern for ourselves and not enough laughter. The pine may be down and its roots all exposed but I am sure he'd rather hear us hooting with mirth than snuffling round like old Blue Hare, all down in the dumps. This is not the last we will see of our friend. Look over there, that is one of the trees that sprang from his stock and all over the

Black Wood there are others growing tall planted by the seeds scattered from the cones his branches produced year by year.

There was a flurry among the smaller animals as the shadow of a kestrel came between them and the sun but quite out of character it called 'Don't be afraid. I am not hunting, my business is with the pine.' Folding his wings he settled.

I come from the birds of prey, the buzzards and hawks. We guard the stories of the woodlands and the old forests. We can tell of the pine martens and the wild cat that knew the shelter of older pines. They are the trees that have stood in Scotland's landscape from before the Ice Age, holding the soil on the hill-sides and ensuring a future for so many other species. Remember the stock from which we all spring; don't forget the centuries in which our ancestors have lived and enjoyed the woodlands; we are all woven together in the bundle of life. Our separate threads were spun from a single fleece of creation, so of course we mourn the pine as one of ourselves, but remember our continuance.

The affirmation of solidarity was broken suddenly by a frisson of deep instinctive fear as the shadow of a Golden Eagle caught their attention. The great bird came diving from the high point where it had been circling. With spread wings and legs outstretched to brake its landing, the Eagle chose the bark of the Pine-trunk for its perch.

'I saw the gap,' he began without introduction. 'This tree has been a signpost for my flights all the years that I have ranged the Forest. I have held its branches as I have found shelter in storms; it has pointed me to the hills in the West.'

Then, as he sensed the prevailing mood of grief, the Eagle spread his wings and glided to a nearby tree-top.

But nothing is lost in the life of the Forest. The ground is enriched by the fallen timber, new trees grow to take the place of the ones that have gone before. Even the memories are not lost. The pine tree watched over generations of rabbits, squirrels and roe deer and cherished the affectionate pictures of their doings. Overlooking all of us, in its turn, is the Will of the World.

I have flown deeper into the sky than any of you and looked down on the earth from great heights. I have watched the rainbow form between the sun and the rain. I have learned that the Will which once sang everything into being, still remembers the whole of the song.

Its echoes reverberate beyond the most distant clouds. Down here the music progresses, but none of the cadences are forgotten, they are all held in the one unending theme. The music of the tree stays as part of the eternal harmony, just as the little animals long gone have their quick patter of notes and the flight of the birds is captured in great arpeggios that the wind plays on the trees. The Song of the Making was not sung once for all but continues through the unending work, as the generations succeed one another and the intricacy of the pattern grows.

Not all the woodland family were ready for such high metaphysics, but they listened respectfully. The Eagle went on,

I once caught the musings of a wise man as he said 'Nothing is lost where everything is glorified'. This has helped my questionings. I have understood better the fierce sword of the lightning, the sadness of a failed brood in the nest and the devastation of floods because of the 'nothing is lost' and I have been comforted by the promise 'everything is glorified'.

We must sing and fly, hunt, feast and mate for the glory of life in its continuance and in gratitude for the Great Song in which all of the past is kept safe. For us the Pine is fallen: it stands and flourishes forever in the Will of the Maker and the celebration of his music.

The Golden Eagle swept from his perch, beating his wings and by their strength and the lift of the wind was gone into the blue of the sky. In spite of the mysterious quality of his words which not all of his listeners fully understood, he seemed to take some of the mourning and sighing of the Forest with him, lifting it into the unclouded realms which his soaring flight explored.

None of the Woodland creatures could remember a time when so many had come together without fear or been so enriched by each other's company as at the gathering for the fall of the great Scots Pine. That itself hinted at a strange mystery, a glimpse of glory, as the Eagle might have said.

8

The Emptying Neighbourhood

The number of funerals to be attended increase as the years go on. A quick glance down the death notices in the morning paper becomes part of the breakfast ritual. The social community made up of one's acquaintances, like an actual neighbourhood is emptying steadily if not dramatically. The loss is felt when there is a joke to tell and the old friend who would have been the natural audience is no longer there to hear it. When there is a memory to be shared, no one is left with whom it resonates. Most important of all is the loss of the confidante upon whose advice one relied. It is no wonder that many old people complain of loneliness. The most devastating loss can be of one's partner. When he or she has died, mourning requires a listening ear. The person with whom it would have been natural to share one's grief, the prime recipient, is the one who has gone, so the sense of absence is redoubled.

There is a further problem which is now becoming more common, arising from divorce. The number of older people who are homeless is increasing, because when a marriage splits up the house cannot be divided and one partner is left without a roof over his or her head.

The social community around a person decreases not only by death or divorce but by retirement. Many of those to whom one turned for professional advice, doctor, dentist, perhaps solicitor, will have been succeeded by others with whom a new relationship has to be built. Another part of the loss are the opportunities for sharing informed comment or grumbling together over a drink when one will not have to explain oneself as to a stranger but begin from common ground. The accustomed sounding board for fresh ideas or new thoughts has gone and either the conversation goes silent or the effort to create new contacts is demanded. But even these will lack the shared background from which confidence in communication grows.

The advice concerning the tasks of grief work still holds good. The truth of the loss and its accompanying pain must be acknowledged in order to find a way forward that does not leave the agenda for life confined to leaning over the graveyard wall or putting flowers on the tomb. This attitude of mind can be disguised as 'loyalty', but in fact it is an unrealistic living in the past. This is particularly true of the bereavement by the loss of a partner. There is a feeling that another marriage devalues all the years that the couple have spent together. Yet the need for a new relationship could be a tribute to the success of the previous experience. Unhappily there is a culture of disapproval which surrounds 'romance' in old age. It may be partly due to vestiges of medieval theology that trace their origins back to St Paul whose advice to widows was that 'it is well for them to remain unmarried as I am. But if they are not practising self-control, they should marry. For it is better to marry than to be aflame with passion' (1 Corinthians 7.8–10).

This needs to be contrasted with the principles of the UN Year of The Older Person which were summed up under the five headings: 'Independence, Participation, Care, Self-fulfilment, Dignity' (Chapter 1). The churches are all struggling to make sense of biblical prohibitions and contemporary living. Do we find 'best practice' in the pages of the New Testament or in the way in which later generations have come to interpret the fundamental command to love, in terms appropriate to their own day and age, using the insights that have accrued from new approaches in psychology or social behaviour?

This is not simply an academic question. It has its effect on the way in which retired people understand themselves after a death and what actions it is permissible to take. The churches are no longer the arbiters of morality, but unconsciously their perceptions condition social attitudes. There is a distaste about admitting that the elderly have sexual responses and this may be expressed either by ignoring or ridiculing them.

As we attempt to understand the problems of the 'emptying

neighbourhood', it will become clear that there is no one solution applicable to all. For some, loss of companionship will be their chief concern and they will need to find ways to fill the gaps. For others, the gift of space will be a source of gratitude. They may be glad of the opportunity to explore areas of inner or outer worlds from which the presence of others inhibited them. Both states can be misunderstood and criticized, the one as lacking in independence, immaturely gregarious; the other may be stigmatized as selfish and uncaring. Might it not be replied that old age should have developed the tolerance that avoids judgements and leaves individuals to find their own solution with which they are comfortable? There is no reason why one stereotype should be assumed to fit all and that those who do not like it are to be bullied into conformity.

For those whom solitude beckons, provision should be made for exploring the inner path. Zen Buddhism has a tradition of stillness which allows an individual to absorb the tranquillity of a sparsely laid out garden or engage in paring down words to form the three lines of a haiku that is rich in meaning. The Christian pattern of spirituality has a similar discipline of withdrawing from burgeoning imagery to find delight in a fast of the mind just as much as in a feast. Old age can be an opportunity for discovering new ways of seeing and savouring. For some this may come naturally. There have always been those who sat and gazed. For others it might be that a body like the University of the Third Age could offer support and instruction in learning, from other generations or other cultures, the art of stilling the outer clamour and finding a stairway into silence. New interests in their turn bring new associates to fill places left empty.

Equally there are new activities which others find helpful. It is not necessary to have a lifelong membership of a bowling club to find that it is a sport that offers a fascination when other more strenuous activities have been outgrown. The river bank with hitherto unknown bird life, herons, cormorants, mallard, widgeon, goosanders, can provide a new subject for study and new friends with whom to undertake it.

Those who wish to remedy their isolation should recognize

that there are many others in the community who share their experiences, feelings and needs. There is, paradoxically, a community of lonely people to be discovered. How an introduction is made requires sensitivity because few people would welcome the attention of another if it came as an act of charity. Hence the importance of discovering a new interest as the common meeting ground. The first principle to establish is that everybody has something to give and something that they need. This can be equally as true in making introductions across generations as between contemporaries. A great many younger people need help in overcoming their inability to read and this can be the gift of an older mentor. The patient, one-to-one supervision offered can achieve what was impossible in the competitive classroom where the under-achiever felt doomed to fail. There are skills and knowledge to be handed on from the retired gardener to a young man just beginning, there are hints and tips that belong to the old days of the apprentice and are in danger of being lost in the more bureaucratic learning of the diploma syllabus at the local college. In a mobile society where a family may have travelled far from its roots, the gift of contact with a substitute grandparent may be uniquely valuable.

Here is an expression of 'family values' that is often overlooked by those who use the slogan as a shorthand for sexual morality. The mutual respect between persons of different generations will do far more to build a wholesome society than the inculcation of any particular code of practice. This could be one of the most important shifts in the understanding of retirement. Through working life the emphasis has been on personal achievement, getting on in the job, saving for the future, buying the car and paying the mortgage. Later the attention may have shifted to the children and their progress. Always there has been one figure or perhaps the family as the focus. For some this remains the case but there is another style of living with a concern for the community. It may be that the remedy for the Emptying Neighbourhood is that people should seek to renew the lost community. This, however, will depend on the assumptions that underlie their image of the neighbourhood.

If we move the picture from an urban to a rural setting, we might imagine the various species that made up the village life originally as a group of competitors for the resources of the surroundings. The farmers would feel that they had to protect their crops from the beasts, birds would prey on insects, there might be a scramble for the plant life as it appeared. The children on the green would resent the cow-pats that soiled their play area. If each were concerned with their own survival, the struggle that ensued would exhibit all the dramatic dimensions of a human soap-opera as they were depicted in a contest, trying to outmanoeuvre each other.

The alternative perception would be of an integrated system in which the activities of each species contributed to the life of all. The insects would make possible the pollination of the plants. The cow-pats would fertilize the ground that in turn fed the cows with grass and meadow flowers, the insects were food for the birds which in turn played a part in the ecological cycle, in particular distributing the seeds from the berries on which they had fed. The song of the integrated and rejuvenating village could become a round in which all could join. The guardians of this ideal should be the elders of the village, and their remedy against the sense of loss would be the recognition that they were themselves moving through a variety of creative roles in a dance that guaranteed the sustainability of life's cycle.

This model of a community which absorbs and repairs loss might begin with a willingness by all who felt bereaved to discover new allies amongst those who remain, to rebuild the damaged framework. If the close family group appears depleted, can it be replaced by a network of cousins whose discovery might be a fresh delight? Are there small groups of like-minded acquaintances who could become a source of new friendship? They might have been drawn together in the first place in support of a charity, by a shared local interest or as members of a church congregation. Welded into a house group their interest in one another could extend far beyond the initial common cause that originally brought them together. One interesting development is the growing number of 'silver surfers', older people who have discovered the Internet. Some 11 per cent of those who are using it, that is to say 1.4 million people, are over 50. Help the Aged has a website. The National Pensioners Convention has urged pensioners to use the Internet for campaigning. 'To get results, we need to get connected', said Jack Jones the former trades union leader and President of the Convention. An organization called 'Hairnet' offers courses to people over 50 in their own homes run by trainers who are themselves over 50. Their publicity includes involvement with the new 'My Hairnet Community'. Is this a possible recruiting ground for the emptying neighbourhood?

Finally there are associations that arise out of a current need that has brought together friends of an earlier time. An example of this comes from a book *Tuesdays with Morrie* mentioned in Chapter 7 as offering a model for the construction of a 'living funeral'. Once the contact had been re-established after a break of 20 years, the former professor, Morrie Schwartz, offered to engage in a quite new undertaking of exploring jointly his reflections on life as he coped with his encroaching disease and viewed the world from a new perspective. Because his former pupil was welcomed as a collaborator, a new tenant moved into the Emptying Neighbourhood that Morrie inhabited and also there was another figure in Albom's landscape. Chance and choice both have a part to play in how we fill our lives or keep them empty.

The reasons that influence our responses lie mostly in our own past and perhaps also the history of our family or culture. As we consider our reactions to the loss that goes with getting older and the remedies that we seek or avoid, it may help to re-examine the roots of our behaviour in the ways that psychological insight has opened up, and at the same time to employ the means that current technology has put at our disposal for historical research. Both disciplines are potentially part of the process of lifelong learning.

In current work with old people there has been a rediscovery of the value of reminiscence. It helps an individual to hold on to a sense of his or her own identity, combating even the inroads of dementia. In telling their story, people define themselves. The patient listener does more to affirm the essence of an individual than some forms of religion which seek to impose a stereotyped response of faith expressed in a fixed credal form. Before people can say that they believe in God, they need to know that he believes in them. St Irenaeus expressed the Christian priority in his statement, 'the glory of God is a living man; and the life of man is the vision of God'. As we understand the value of the individual and his or her contribution to the pattern of creation, we begin the journey of exploration into the nature and meaning of God. The primary encounter with divinity is as we discover the 'Thou', the richness of humanity, in a fellow human being. The depth of encounter goes on to colour every other relationship. To think in this way is to find a new depth in our membership of the whole community. This leads on to a fresh experience of God. The Buddhist teacher Thich Nhat Hanh has written

> The tradition of joining our palms together and bowing when we meet someone is very beautiful. Millions of men and women in Asia greet each other this way every day . . . To join our palms in a lotus bud is to offer the person standing before us a fresh flower . . . When our respect is sincere we remember that he or she has the nature of a Buddha, the nature of awakening. (Nhat Hanh, 1993)

The thought which goes with his gesture is

> A lotus for you
> A Buddha to be.

In Christian symbolism this can be translated in to a handshake with the accompanying words

> Strength and compassion from my hand
> for you, Earth-sharer, God-bearer.

Such an idea can influence and transform many encounters which might otherwise be deadening. For instance the question of how we respond to the increasing number of those who suffer from the various forms of dementia and in particular from Alzheimer's disease is a specialist matter, but the truth remains that however much the individual has departed from his or her former self we need to seek ways to accord to people the dignity of their present autonomy and their past history. In doing this we will be much assisted if we can hold on to the quality of their remembered life. We become the guardians of the story that they have forgotten. For the Alzheimer's sufferer, the patterns of cerebral learning have virtually disappeared but there often remains an emotional capacity for receiving the gift of warmth and affection. What they may not have been able to achieve by cognitive skills, indeed may almost have used their intellect to avoid, may be enhanced as they are taken into a second infancy surrounded with affectionate care that accepts them unconditionally.

This often requires a reversal of roles between generations. The once-child must parent the former elder. This is helped by the recollection that however much the older sufferer seems to be bereft of formerly discerned qualities, the truth remains that this is someone who is still an 'Earth-sharer' and a 'God-bearer'. The same may be true of a person who has suffered a stroke with the impairments of speech and mobility that it brings.

Meanwhile for the alert individual, part of the process of reminiscence can link to the more serious work of self-understanding that comes from the recovery of childhood memories. Snapshots in the mind recalling long-forgotten events or unacknowledged feelings can be a source of spontaneous insight. For some this may link to unfinished analytical work. I remember Dr Jock Sutherland, the former director of the Tavistock Institute for Human Relations in London telling me, a few months before his death, how he had recently come to a new area of insight that helped him understand his relationship with his father many years before. This he felt had currently allowed him to write with much greater freedom and fluency. I fancy that this referred specifically to his remarkable biography of Dr Ronald Fairbairn, the ground-breaking Edinburgh psychoanalyst that he had recently published. What I took from the conversation was admiration for somebody who after a lifetime of active achievement and inner exploration was still committed to the process of self-discovery and had no feeling that he had come to an end of learning. This was for me a witness to the eternity of the spirit in every person. I have taken his lesson to heart and found great profit in reviewing my own childhood, especially through the recovery of long-forgotten incidents, and seeking to find their meaning for me today.

Another source of insight in old age is provided by grand-children. Observing the patterns of their upbringing and responses, we are challenged to reflect on our own contrasting experiences. I look at my own grandchildren and remember myself at their age, I recall old hurts and delights, recover forgot-ten incidents and in the process discern more of the assumptions by which my upbringing was shaped. Grandchildren are among the many tools that old age provides to help us engage with Socrates' ideal of self-discovery which he encapsulated in the aphorism that 'The unexamined life is not worth living'.

Alongside the work of personal exploration, there is a role for history in an understanding of the corporate identity of any generation. Currently there is a particular interest in genealogy, assisted as it is by the internet with websites dedicated to the research of family history. It is more important for the would-be scholar to appreciate the context of the events rather than the details. G. K. Chesterton once said scornfully to an historian whom he believed was too obsessed by facts: 'Why, you could not even walk across a room like a man in the Middle Ages!' Imagination can be much more important than detail when we need to immerse ourselves in a context historically or geo-graphically remote.

If one is to celebrate the centenary of a building, the narrator needs to know what was going on while the work was in progress, what the builders talked about at their lunch break and what was the news of the day. To understand and illuminate any moment in history requires an imagination that can collect the diverse strands and show how they affect each other. The ideal end to be achieved in gathering memories is for all the contributors to feel the unique difference that each made to the whole. Everything is worth recalling.

With such an understanding of the past, there will always be new contacts to be found who have contributed to the life of greater society and who will be ready to take their part in renewing the fellowship of one's personal 'neighbourhood'. As long as any communication is possible, a human being is never alone. There will always be those who want to hear his story and to tell him theirs. It requires the confidence to believe that this is the case and to make the contacts that break the isolation.

There is, however, a greater depth for each person to uncover in their inner world. We have already reflected on the difference between the most basic or ontological fear that various types of people carry round inside them. Why do some fear condemnation, others meaninglessness and a final group, annihilation? There is at least one way of telling their different stories that might offer an explanation. This goes back to the observations of Dr John Bowlby, another distinguished child analyst of the post-war years who practised at the Tavistock Clinic in London. He built a now widely accepted theory around the experience of attachment as an infant grew up. In a way he is describing the kind of people that the child found as the first inhabitants of the neighbourhood or village in which he grew up, but ultimately it is arguable that this is what conditioned his attitude to the opposite experience of detachment in old age.

The theory is based on some carefully planned experiments. Working within a relatively controlled environment, it has been observed that there are three distinct styles in which a child becomes attached to his parents and particularly his mother. As studied within a clinical setting they fall into one of three categories, either securely attached, ambivalently attached or avoidant. Part of the experimental basis for these conclusions was to introduce a mother and child to a strange situation and observe how the child responded when his mother got up, left him and then returned. The doctor concerned with structuring the experiment described it like this:

I thought, Well, let's work it all out; we'll have the mother and baby together in a strange environment with a lot of toys to invite exploration. Then we'll introduce a stranger when the mother's still there and see how the baby responds. Then we'll have a separation situation where the mother leaves the baby with the stranger. How does the baby respond to her departure? And when the mother returns, how does the baby respond to the reunion? But since the stranger was in the room during the first departure, maybe we'd better have an episode in which the mother leaves the baby entirely alone. Then we could see whether the return of the stranger would lessen whatever distress has occurred. Finally we'll have another reunion with the mother. (Mary Ainsworth quoted in Roberts, 1994: 151)

The secure children coped with a minimum of distress which was quickly assuaged on the mother's return. The ambivalently attached children were extremely distressed by the separations and eagerly wanted their mothers back and yet resisted them on their return. Love and hate seemed to be struggling for dominance.

Much more concerning were the avoidant children. They did not immediately respond to the mother's return but seemed to have developed a defence against the distress of separation. It was as though they had already learned to interpret absence as rejection and employed an emotional cut-off to disguise their hurt and anger even from themselves. This was parallel with the behaviour observed in older children after a long and depriving separation. (Roberts, 1994: 158)

There is no time to enter more fully into the description of all the findings. The point of introducing the account of the experiment is to lead in to the fact that Bowlby attributed to such experiences the formation within each individual of an 'internal working model'.

'Through sucking, clinging, following, smiling, crying and when older, by going to mother when in physical or emotional distress or simply when he wants attention, the child explores his relationships and builds a model of the way they work. The internal working model . . . reflects the child's relationship history, codifying the behaviours that belong to an intimate relationship and defining how he will feel about himself when he is closely involved with another person.' (Roberts, 1994: 209)

As far as we are concerned the question is: 'what effect does the internal working model have upon styles of learning and development in old age and upon handling the approach of death?' Might the securely attached person find it possible to slip off the lap of the nurturing environment and go to play in a new place with only a modicum of anxiety? Would the avoidant child grow up into an adult who gave no external sign of grief as he felt life slipping away and go, denying all emotion, 'into that good night'. His unconscious decision might be to let no one come near him or sense his distress. This response would, in fact, increase the load of grief, and perhaps guilt, carried by others when he died. There have been cultures where such a withdrawal would have been commended as variously 'heroic', 'Christian' or 'stoic'. We are more likely to categorize it as flight from the opportunity of being an emotionally mature human being. Dynamically understood, such behaviour would be consistent with a pattern of living that arose out of the person's original internal working model which took him into a world of isolation, because loss had been so devastating an experience that it was safer to live alone than risk repeating the pain. In childhood such a person might appear independent, self-contained and undemanding and therefore be regarded as 'well-adjusted'. In later life he will look for little help in handling his emotions, resist offers of co-operation or supervision, be slow to make close friendships and even in a marriage may be undemonstrative and when occasion arises prefer to grieve alone. Between the securely attached and the avoidant child lies the anxiously attached. Would he or she be the person who needed pastoral reassurance as the fundamental anxiety of imminent death was experienced but who still remained in touch, obeying Dylan Thomas' injunction to 'Rage, rage against the dying of the light'?

In any reflection about death we need to be aware that while other forms of loss call in question our response, that is always from the stand-point of an active handling of the loss. The self continues to exist as bereaved, diminished, suffering but always as part of the scene. Death is the moment when that core self ceases to be. The anxiety this arouses is different in kind from any other loss.

But how do Bowlby's findings help an understanding of Tillich's list of three basic fears, condemnation, meaninglessness and annihilation? These also can claim to be the result of careful observation and can be tested in any small group of people who are prepared to make an honest declaration of their emotions. The securely attached child is made anxious by his mother's departure and makes overtures to her when she returns. The fear which he has exhibited on her departure may simply be a concern about separation, but if we explore it in terms of the unspoken thoughts, we must ask if he was thinking that he was responsible for his mother's departure and maybe he will be blamed on her eagerly anticipated return. He greets her with a warm welcome, inviting her to respond in kind. Does this correlate with Tillich's ultimate anxiety about condemnation or rejection?

The ambivalently attached child greets the returning mother with resentment. 'How dare you abandon me!' This correlates with the anxiety about meaninglessness. If we find our being in relationships, following the African proverb 'People are people through other people', to be abandoned even for a brief period puts the child's meaning at risk. No wonder that he is angry at being subjected to such a threat. But even if anger replaces love in his response to her return, the relationship is still sustained on the principle 'that it is better to be wanted for murder than not to be wanted at all'. The struggle is to establish a framework of meaning.

The threat of annihilation derives from a fear that nobody cares or is in relationship. If that is the case, then ultimately personal existence will drop into the abyss of nothingness. This resonates with the experience of the avoidant child. He has already built into his world-view the conviction that nobody will respond, there is nothing to appeal to and so he has withdrawn into himself. If anything of him is to survive, it depends on resources within. If death is now going to demolish this last bastion of his inner core, then there is nothing left.

If there is any validity in such a construct we need to ask how these ontological anxieties can be met, since they will be powerfully present in the experience of the Emptying Neighbourhood. As the supportive friends go and the survivor finds him or herself increasingly dependent, the patterns of childhood seem to reassert themselves. The stereotype of the fretful, cantankerous old person has been exploited by generations of dramatists, from the Elizabethan stage to the contemporary television sitcom. Does the humour consist in watching the old person revert to type and act out the conflicts of childhood when he experienced for the first time the frustrations that are being repeated in the geriatric ward or residential home? How far are the responses to the nurses or care staff a repeat of what happened between himself and a mother who was too busy, harassed or preoccupied to give all the attention that he felt that he desperately needed?

If this is a valid way to make sense of the anxieties of old age and the way that we respond to them, then there is an urgent case for training to be given to those who have responsibility for the welfare of senior citizens. For some it may be in their role as volunteers; for others who engage with them as part of the statutory services, in whatever way they are involved the care which they offer will be greatly enhanced by the trouble that they have taken to equip themselves not simply to deal with surface issues but to encounter the individuals in every aspect of their personality. In this way they too will be acknowledging the emptying neighbourhood and have a concern for dealing with its loneliness.

Reverting to the thoughts of Chapter 4, 'Permission to Play', we might find that another line of approach was, at least for some, not the high sounding motivation of social service but rather the enjoyment of human company. Through agencies as diverse as the University of the Third Age and the Bingo hall they might be echoing the invitation of the young child's 'Come and play!' as they arrived to fill in their cards at the caller's behest, learn to listen to a Mozart concerto or join in Scottish country dancing according to taste. It may require quite a brave revision of roles, but the Neighbourhood in Old Age does not have to remain depopulated.

9

The Politics of Age

We began with an examination of the facts of the demographic shift that has seen life expectancy rise dramatically, changed the structure of world population and given increased voting power to older citizens.

We have argued that society needs a new understanding of what it means to be old, so that the elderly can value themselves and find an assured place in society. This will need to be reflected in political decisions, so that younger generations can look forward to a life that progresses to a fruitful and secure retirement built on the three elements of inner assurance, an acceptance by the community and adequate financial provision. These will depend in their turn on personal confidence, societal attitudes and legislative decisions. The various fields of health, including birth and death, the provision of care and finally work, environment and life-styles all require specific treatment.

There was a time of medical innocence when birth, good health and death were believed to lie primarily in the gift of God, reflecting his good pleasure or his judgement. Gradually with advancing knowledge and skill, healing first acquired a scientific base in medical practice; later it became possible that conception could be avoided or arranged; finally death could be held at bay and lost its arbitrary power.

The management of the life processes has not been universally welcomed. Sometimes a demarcation dispute has arisen between the religious and medical practitioners. Primitive healing arts resided in religious shrines and medical claims seemed to usurp the role of the priests who guarded the rituals and perhaps the rudimentary herbal lore. More especially this has been true of the issues of birth and death. As the situation has changed, with their advanced techniques and pharmacology doctors are accused of playing God. The penalty is that when exaggerated expectations are disappointed, the doctors are liable to be pursued at law by aggrieved patients or relatives on the grounds that they have not tried hard enough to succeed in their role. Sometimes in spite of their best efforts we die, at other times we complain that they have been over-zealous in their efforts to revive a patient who seemed ready to go. On such an occasion it could have seemed preferable to allow a natural process of infection to take over and not to intervene with aggressive techniques of resuscitation or the use of antibiotics. The issue then is where the decision-making process lies. If as individuals we have spent our life moving towards increased autonomy, is there a moment when that should be reversed and surrendered either to medical judgement or moral principles dictated by others? Professor Hans Küng offers a critique of this view from a Christian perspective:

> Precisely because I am convinced that another new life is intended for me, as a Christian I see myself given freedom by God to have a say in my dying, a say about the nature and time of my death – in so far as this is granted me. Certainly the question of a dignified dying may not in any case be reduced to the question of active help in dying: but it may not be detached from that either. A dignified dying also includes responsibility for dying in keeping with human dignity – not out of mistrust or arrogance towards God but out of unshakeable trust in God who is not a sadist but the merciful God whose grace proves eternal. (Küng, 1995: 39)

Former generations could find consolation in the notion that all the great issues depended on God. Death was his choice so they wrote on the tombstone 'Thy will be done' and asked none of the complicated questions which we have learned to associate with mourning.

Similarly the blessings of a long life were assumed to be undisputed. When the Jews returned to Palestine after their exile in Babylon, around 540 BC there was a sense of a new world begun. There was an outburst of prophetic writing associated with the school of the Second Isaiah. From among this group appeared an ecstatic hymn of hope. For the author this crystallized around both an end to infant mortality and the gift of longevity:

> No child will ever again die in infancy;
> nor old man fail to live out his span of life.
> He who dies at a hundred is just a youth,
> and if he does not attain a hundred, he is thought accursed!
> My people will build houses and live in them
> plant vineyards and eat their fruit.
> They will not build for others to live in,
> or plant for others to eat;
> They will be as long lived as a tree,
> and my chosen ones will enjoy the fruit of their labour.
> They will not toil to no purpose,
> or raise children for misfortune
> because they and their issue after them
> are a race blessed by the Lord.
> (Isaiah 65.18–23)

This kind of thinking has formed religious assumptions down the centuries. In our day scientific medicine has given us a new perspective. At least in part the decisions about birth and death have become privatized. Individuals are claiming the right to choose if and when they will have children, and similarly to say when their life has so far deteriorated in quality that they can decide that it is time to go. Society is beginning to think the unthinkable and to face the rationing of health-care on the basis of age.

There has been a knee-jerk reaction to block any legislation which seeks to rationalize the situation, often led by the Christian laity or clergy. This is only one side of a debate which needs to be held so that adults can wrestle with the implications of death during the time of their health. There was a time when the Christian tradition encouraged its members to live with the presence of death, sometimes placing a skull on the dinner table as a reminder. They prayed that they would not die suddenly and unprepared.

This has continued in European thought (see page 36), but now needs to be addressed from the new perspectives provided by medical advances. As individuals reflect on what choices have opened, there is a place for personal decisions so that they do not leave agonizing choices to the family or the doctor.

If the process of dying involves a long-drawn-out terminal illness rather than a sudden death, are there any provisions to be made for managing this and for whose benefit are they to be made? Nobody dies to themselves, even if the act of dying is a solitary one. It affects others by sorrow, guilt or example. Just as Dr Donald Winnicott observed that there is no such thing as a solitary baby, always a nursing couple (even when the mother is physically absent), so too with a death the social complex is significant, even if it is not physically present, and at a death proper cognisance needs to be taken of the network of involved persons. The care for those who mourn, the legacy of memories, the emotions which will influence the grief process are all part of dying and, when given proper attention, can make the event more or less creative. The very fact of exploring such possibilities is in itself helpful. They draw the sting of death which can become such a bogey if it is treated as an unmentionable horror. We have absorbed the aphorism 'Never say die' too literally and it has ministered to a damaging taboo.

The use of advance directives can reverse this silence and encourage an open and healthy conversation about what dying might entail. They strike a note of encouragement for a dialogue between patient and doctor. It must be recognized that this demands a high level of emotional commitment from the doctor. For her or him too there is the challenge of facing the personal issue of mortality. Nevertheless the meeting on a human level can make an important contribution to the exchange between the partners in a therapeutic relationship which is not simply one way. Advance directives also open the possibility for a discussion between other persons involved, the family of the dying patient, friends and all those who will be affected by the death. If there can be an open exchange about what is to be expected they will have less cause to fear the experience of their own death. Too much of the discussion of this issue has been in terms of the individual. A positive and fearless attitude to death can not only be an enhancement of the dignity of the dying person, letting him or her hold on to autonomy to the end, but also an opportunity for others to be less afraid of the whole life process that leads to death and personally find a new maturity.

One of the groups who might gain most from an opening of the dialogue concerning life and death are the doctors themselves, since this is an issue that they handle as a necessary part of their work, particularly as GPs and consultants. As long as death remains a forbidden topic, they will carry the projection of the patient's hope, becoming the miracle worker who will exorcise the demon by potent pills or surgical procedures. It is flattering to be credited with messianic powers but the cost is that we crucify the messiah who fails. The patient may reject the doctor who cannot deliver the impossible. The mourning relatives may use him or the hospital as the focus for the anger that is always near the surface in unresolved grief.

My own mother's death helped me to reflect on the gifts that an aware and dedicated doctor can bring to a whole family and not only the dying patient. My mother was in her mid-eighties and had for many years suffered such chronic rheumatic pain that she declared she could never stay in bed for even a day because of the ensuing distress. We had never formally discussed her death; there were no advance directives around; but she had made it clear to my father, my sister and myself that she would not wish to die in hospital. She suffered a stroke and lost her speech and mobility. Our GP visited regularly and it became clear that any hint of improvement was massively offset by the pain from her rheumatic joints. From the beginning we discussed the situation with the doctor and his commitment was that my mother should not be allowed to suffer. Since my parents had moved next to the vicarage, my wife and I could go in and out all the time. My sister flew back from Singapore. After some three weeks we faced the fact that my mother was deteriorating: the prognosis was that she might last a little longer, but her body language and her distress were saying that she was ready to go.

We considered the possibility of finding a bed in a local convent hospital but the prospect so horrified her that the option was rejected.

The whole family joined our doctor in conference. We all agreed that my mother should not be allow to suffer unduly. As the pain from her arthritis became increasingly distressing the doctor said, 'I think that the time has come to slow things up.' He administered an injection that overcame the restlessness of her distressed body and that evening she died with a great sense of peace and her family round her.

There was no way in which I could have encouraged my mother's continuance like a wounded animal. For a day or two I was assailed with doubts about whether as a priest I should have had the faith to attempt a healing that was beyond medical power. I quickly recognized that this was a fantasy of my own omnipotence. I have remained deeply grateful to our doctor for his careful treatment of the whole family at a time of crisis, for his honesty and his compassion. I hope that out of the transaction he took away some enrichment. I pray that there will be someone like him around when I come to die. But this is not a matter of chance or good luck. The carefully thought-out texts of advance directives and the change in culture that has produced them open the possibility for securing a responsible, humane, life-enhancing and I believe Christian discussion that points the way forward. It requires that society should endorse the validity of such a procedure probably by carefully thought-out legislation.

We have already raised the issue of pensions, state or private, the provision of housing, the costs of care, the protection of old people from abuse by those who should be concerned for their well-being. So many of the problems raised stem from financial difficulties. How does the sufferer from Alzheimer's disease receive the care he or she needs? Will the patient exhaust the carer's compassion or the family savings? These are the recommendations argued out in the Sutherland Report which still await the political decision to implement them.

Meanwhile legislative action is required to address the incidence of elder abuse which is slowly achieving prominence as a subject in contemporary society. The romantic fiction of generous affection as the mark of family life is challenged by the facts which we often prefer not to hear. The issue is given graphic expression in a campaign mounted by Age Concern. A poster shows a granny figure seated while behind her stands a young man. Words beside him read

'I_____my gran'
    Insert as appropriate
            Hit
            Bully
            Steal from
            Rape
            Neglect
            Humiliate

It is not enough to highlight the stories of abuse or to react with horror. Political action with the provision of funds for specific work is needed. This will include making available police time with special units as for Child Protection. From time to time stories emerge from residential care homes which tell of abuse by staff, and Age Concern Scotland has gone on record with the statement: 'We believe that the abuse of older people is one of the most serious and hidden problems facing older people today.' Britain is slowly catching up with good practice pioneered in Canada. The question is whether public perception sees this as the kind of cancer in society that requires legislation to combat it.

The other needs of old people have been mentioned: their inclusion in the working community so that they do not feel marginalized, the provision of adequate transport so that they can maintain contact with families and friends, suitable housing which recognizes disabilities and is designed to accommodate them. Finally there is the disputed agenda of the pension where prudent Treasury officials seek to balance an acceptable level of taxation against the fury of those who see their small state pension, where it is their only income, as a form of institutionalized elder abuse.

Earlier in this book Dylan Thomas' poem 'Do not go gentle into that good night' was quoted. It is full of resentment and frustration at the wastefulness of life:

> Do not go gentle into that good night
> Old men should burn and rave at close of day
> Rage, rage against the dying of the light.

At the end of Bunyan's *Pilgrim's Progress* all the company who come to the River have a sense of accomplishment and therefore go over singing. For some, religious faith is part of the equation but this carries no guarantee. There have been saints like Francis of Assisi who died with a riot of song and shocked his more austere successor Brother Elias. There have also been women and men who have professed no creed but set sail with high hopes on a wind of satisfaction. Equally a life of credal orthodoxy can precede a bitter death.

Retirement offers the challenge to review our journey, come to terms with what has been and to find the music which will teach us the dance or the song which will carry us forward. If we have chosen well it will perhaps leave others a reel to follow or a chorus to sing that recruits others to the cause we have served.

Further Reading

Age Resource: The Experience of a Lifetime (Age Concern information pack), London: Age Resource, 1999.

Alone But Not Isolated: Responding to the Communication Needs of Older People Utilising New Technology and Older Volunteers: Report of a Research Study in Six European Countries, London: Retired and Senior Volunteer Programme (RSVP), 1999.

Beattie, Alistair et al, *Involving Older People*, London: Age Concern England, 2000.

Boaz, Annette, Hayden, Carol and Bernard, Miriam, *Attitudes and Aspirations of Older People: A Review of the Literature*, Leeds: Corporate Document Services, 1999.

Bridging the Generations: An Overview of Intergenerational Volunteering in Scotland, Stirling: Volunteer Development Scotland, 1996.

Brown, Rosemary, *Good Non Retirement Guide 2000*, London: Kogan Page, 2000.

Bryden, Betty, Harbert, Wally and Little, Alan, *We Want to Give Something Back*, London: Community Service Volunteers, 1998.

Clark, George and Herman, Matt, *Keeping Active? A Report Documenting a Feasibility Study Looking at the Use of Senior Health Mentors to Promote Physical Activity Amongst Their Peers in Midlothian*, Edinburgh: Lothian Health Board, 1999.

Dean, Judy and Morton, Margaret, *A Chance to Help: Survey of Later Life Volunteers in Scotland*, Stirling: Volunteer Development Scotland, 1995.

Dench, Sally and Regan, Jo, *Learning in Later Life: Motivation and Impact*, London: Department for Education and Employment, 2000.

Dingle, Alan, *A Guide for Absolute Beginners: A View of the Voluntary Sector for Retired Business and Professional People*, London: REACH, 1995.

Engaging Older Volunteers in Schools: A Guide and Ideas Handbook for Teachers in Scotland, Edinburgh: Age Concern Scotland, 1997.

Engaging Older Volunteers in Schools: School Training Pack for PAT Sessions, Aberdeen: Aberdeenshire Council, Age Concern Scotland, 1997.

Further Reading

Family Friends: A Program Guide, Washington: National Council on the Aging, 1996.

Fifty Plus Volunteering: Volunteering Development Manual, Glasgow: Engage Scotland, 1998.

Forster, Jane, *Potential of a Lifetime*, Dunfermline: Carnegie United Kingdom Trust, 1997.

Forster, Jane, *Potential of a Lifetime: Research Summary No. 1: Study of Older Volunteers in 25 Organisations*, Dunfermline: Carnegie United Kingdom Trust, 1998.

Guide to Good Volunteering in Scotland, Glasgow: Age Concern Scotland, Engage Scotland, 1996.

Harbert, Wally, *Part of the Team: Partnerships Between Professionals and Older Volunteers in Primary Care*, London: RSVP, Help the Aged, 1998.

Hill, Catherine et al, *Social Focus on Older People*, London: Stationery Office, 1999.

Later Life Volunteers: Equal Opportunities and Good Practice, Stirling: Volunteer Development Scotland, 1995.

Lifelong Action: A Guide to Recruiting and Retaining Older Volunteers, London: Home Office, Active Community Unit, 1999.

Morton, Margaret and Owen, Eleanor, *Older People, the Environment and Voluntary Activity: A Short Report of a Focus Group Study Conducted in Scotland During the Spring of 1998*, Glasgow: Engage Scotland, Age Concern Scotland, 1998.

Niyazi, Filiz, *Volunteering by Older People: A Route to Opportunity*, London: National Centre for Volunteering, 1996.

Releasing the Resource: Older Adults as Helpers in Learning Processes, Barcelona: European Association for the Education of Adults, 1997.

Scales, Jonathan and Pahl, Ray, *Future Work and Lifestyles: Final Report*, London: Millennium Debate of the Age, 1999.

Scott, Helena, *The Making of Good Practice: Changing Attitudes to Ageing Through Action*, Dublin: Age and Opportunity, 1997.

Trans Age Action: Based on the US Foster Grandparent Programme: The Evaluation of the Three-Year Pilot Phase 1995–1998, London Age Concern England, 1999.

Winning the Generation Game: Improving Opportunities for People aged 50–65 in Work and Community Activity: A Summary, London: Cabinet Office, Performance and Innovation Unit, 2000.

Worsley, Richard, *Future Work and Lifestyles: Interim Report*, London: Millennium Debate of the Age, 1997.